The Elegance of
Silk Ribbon

MILNER CRAFT SERIES

The Elegance *of*
Silk Ribbon

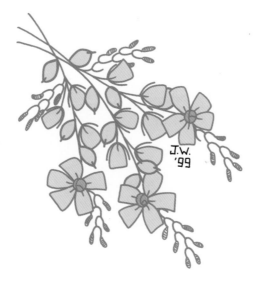

Joan Watters

First published in 2000 by
Sally Milner Publishing Pty Ltd
PO Box 2104
Bowral NSW 2576
Australia

© Joan Watters, 2000

Design Ken Gilroy
Photography Tim Conley
Illustrations Leslie Grifffiths
Styling Robyn Wilson
Editing Donna Hennessy

Printed in Hong Kong

National Library of Australia Cataloguing-in-Publication data:
Watters, Joan
The Elegance of Silk Ribbon Embroidery

ISBN 1-86351-251-9

1. Silk Ribbon Embroidery I. Title (Series: Milner Craft Series)

Contents

DEDICATION

I would like to dedicate this book to two wonderful friends of mine. The two people are Helen O'Neil and her late husband, Mark. Helen, we have been friends for a long time and I know if ever I need you, you are always there for me, for which I thank you very much. Mark was taken from us at a very early age last year, 26th April 1999. Helen and Mark have allowed me to have their beautiful home for the photography for all of my three books. Mark was a wonderful person. It is tragic when someone is taken from us while still in the prime of his life. Mark, we miss you very much and I hope you will appreciate me dedicating this book to you, which I think blooms and represents you. My daughter Peta has written the next section especially for you Mark.

"Mark was an incredibly unique person who blessed the lives of each individual he met. Whether you needed a shoulder to cry on, a lending hand, or merely someone to talk to in times of need, Mark was always there, willing to help strangers despite the internal battles which he courageously fought against in order to see the dawn of each new day. He was a true humanitarian and believer of the family unit. His true passion for life lay within his wife Helen and sons Sam and James who provided an endless stream of love to Mark's heart, which in turn gave him the greatest honour of all – unity. Yet when cancer threatened Mark's life, he illustrated his pure determination and bravery to beat the internal enemy who sought to snatch his life away from the ones who loved him the most. Mark fought like a soldier to the very end, when finally he could endure no more and was forced to wave the white flag as he submitted his life to the enemy force.

Mark, you shone light on my world when it was dark,
you gave me strength when I was weak,
you gave me hope when there was none.
All I can say is Thank You... You may now fly free... angel".

ACKNOWLEDGMENTS

I have some wonderful companies I have to thank for their support with this book and for all the projects I embroider.

To DMC Australia, thank you for donating all the silk ribbons, stranded threads and fabrics. To all the staff who always praise my embroideries when I go out to see them. Thank you for all your kind words of support.

To Kacoonda, thank you Kathy for all your donations of silk ribbons, silk threads and all your hard work dying the colours I have designed with you. Thank you for all those last minute materials I usually need yesterday. I have been using your threads now for quite a few years and I still love them as much as I did when I first started embroidering with them.

To Louise from Rajmahal threads, thank you for all your kind words about my embroideries and the donations of your threads.

To Imperial Framing, especially Alex, for the wonderful framing jobs you have done for me.

To the wonderful lady who paints the porcelain dolls to match my embroidery. Thank you for all your hard work and how you share your enthusiasm with me when I come up with a doll idea in a rush.

To Helen, who lets me have the photography taken in her beautiful home. Helen you are a wonderful friend and you know how much I appreciate you lending me your home. This is the third book for which I have had the photos taken in your home.

To Robyn and Tim who do the photography and styling. Robyn and Tim, you make my embroideries look wonderful. I love the way you present my embroidery and we all know how hard we work for those two days of photography. The photography and styling in this book makes my embroidery bloom.

I would like to thank a lovely young lady, Elizabeth Gwalter, from Express Publications for writing my Life in Stitches for my author's profile.

To Sally Milner Publishing, Libby and Ian thank you for having the confidence in my embroidery to enable me to produce another book. This is my third book with your company and there are still more books to come I can assure you.

To my wonderful daughter Peta, I could not write any of my books without your loving support. If you did not turn the computer on and off for me I would have to write all my books by hand, as I am computer illiterate. I can type and save and that is my limit with a computer. I would much rather have a needle and thread in my hand than learn how to use the computer. I thank you for all your moral support as well, you make me keep going, life would not be worth living if you were not by my side. You are my best friend and I thank you baby from the bottom of my heart.

Joan Watters is one of those special people who can not only see beauty in the world around her but can capture these images in thread, ribbons and fabric. Her original embroidery pieces will be beautiful heirlooms of tomorrow.

Some people spend their whole life trying to discover their special talents. Joan Watters is not one of those people. She was lucky enough to have discovered her passion for embroidery at the early age of five, sitting by her mother's side and stitching buttons onto fabric for fun (and to amuse herself because she was an only child). By the time she was nine, she had progressed to traditional fine embroidery. By the tender age of eleven, she was sewing clothes for herself and her mother. It seems, a life of using her hands was planned for her even though Joan inherited a family problem of arthritis. Joan is very determined her arthritis will not interfere with her love of designing and embroidering.

When Joan was sixteen, she began working for a dressmaker in Brisbane. Although she stitched wedding and party dresses, which were regularly featured in the social pages of The Australian Women's Weekly, her boss designed and cut out all the patterns. Joan was clever enough to watch her boss as she worked and picked up a life time of skills which were to serve her well in the years to come. Joan started her own dress-making business at the ripe age of nineteen and continued the business for seventeen years. The last dress, and the finish of Joan's dressmaking life, was a beautiful christening gown which can be seen in Joan's last book Heirlooms of Tomorrow in Wool Embroidery. What a lovely way to end a dressmaking career!

Joan wrote her first book in 1994, called Creative Wool Embroidery; another book in 1998, called Heirlooms of Tomorrow in Wool Embroidery and now, The Elegance of Silk Ribbon. This is not the end of Joan's writing, as there are two more books on the way.

Joan Watters

9

INTRODUCTION

This is my first silk ribbon book and I hope you enjoy this book as much as you have enjoyed my wool embroidery books. The projects in this book cater for the beginner and the experienced embroiderer. Some projects are very involved but there are many projects which are for the first time silk ribbon embroiderer. If you have never embroidered with silk ribbon before, do not be scared. If you can embroider with wool, you can embroider with silk ribbon. The other good thing about silk ribbon embroidery is, you can make a mess on the back of your embroidery if you wish. Of course, those who wish to make the back and front the same can go ahead. The only thing you cannot do in silk ribbon is tie knots to start off, this is a no no in my book. Silk ribbon embroidery is quick (the same as wool) and the same rule applies with silk ribbon as with wool, do not pull the silk ribbon tight.

I have to thank my Dad for taking me out with him as a little girl and telling me the names of flowers and helping him in the garden. You see, my Dad in his early days was a gardener. My love of flowers started a long time ago. I also have to thank my Mother for showing me at a very early age how to embroider. Sadly, I cannot thank my parents as they are both deceased, but maybe they can see the results. In this book you will see a wedding photo of my parents in the wedding cushion, coathanger and wedding card. This is my way of saying thank you to them. I am trying to hand my knowledge down to my daughter. Peta is a very good wool embroiderer and I have also taught her silk ribbon embroidery. Peta is in her last year of school and will sit her HSC this year and one of her subjects is Design & Technology which I am sure she will do very well in.

I have only been designing wool and silk ribbon embroidery for seven years now and I have never been taught how to design, it just comes when I have a needle in my hand. I design in an unusual way, I start with a blank piece of fabric and I just start and the designs just come to me once I start embroidering. I sometimes look at the designs when I have finished and think how did I come up with this design, but I can assure you all my designs are originals. In the past two years, I have embroidered with silk ribbon constantly. I have embroidered all the silk ribbon samples for DMC Australia, and I have also embroidered projects regularly for Embroidery and Cross Stitch, Country Craft and Handmade magazines. I love my work because I embroider a new project nearly every day.

I have so much to offer the embroiderer and I know how much embroiderers enjoy my work because they ring me so often and tell me, for this I thank you. I still have an enormous amount of designs to be embroidered yet. I am so lucky, the designs keep coming and I never cease to amaze myself with every new project I embroider. I have this ability to turn my thoughts into an embroidery. I have another book on the way, using stranded thread. This is a new field for me because in the last year or so I have been embroidering with DMC stranded thread. I have had some lovely feedback from students who love embroidering my designs using this medium.

My last words to all you wonderful embroiderers are, thank you for purchasing my new book and "Happy Stitching."

Getting

Started

MATERIALS

The fabric you choose to embroider will make or break your embroidery. I am an ex-dressmaker and had my own business for seventeen years and I know my fabrics. I don't worry how much the fabric costs because if I am going to embroider a beautiful embroidery, I can assure you I am not going to use cheap fabric. I usually use: pure silk dupion fabric, good quality damask, silk satin or a good quality satin, Belfast pure linen, Quakers cloth (which is a linen and cotton blend), pure wool flannel, Olympia Crewel linen or a good quality velveteen and wool blanketing.

As a rule, I back most of my silk ribbon embroidery with a cotton voile. I think the voile makes a better embroidery and you can jump across the back of your embroidery without seeing the outline on the front of your embroidery. Even so, I do only make small jumps on the back of my embroidery. The voile also closes the hole in the fabric made by the larger embroidery needle. The voile rule can be broken when you embroider on wool blanketing and wool flannel. I did break the rule once in this book on a simple Lavender bag because the stitches used were mainly surface stitches and I wanted this project to be something you could embroidery quickly. See rules can be broken, do what I say not what I do, I am the boss remember.

The range of silk ribbon threads is increasing all the time. I have embroidered with a vast range of silk ribbons and it is very hard to say which one is the best. They are all good in there own special way. I have designed a few colours with Kacoonda and of course I tend to use them, naturally because I designed them. 8J is one from Kacoonda, broken down it means 8 Joan. It is a beautiful green which goes with everything. No 4 is another one, and is a variegated cream. This colour also goes with everything. I am noted for my tone on tone embroidery much to the delight of the photographer and stylist. I have also used a lot of Bucilla silk ribbons in this book because they are available in most places and they have a nice colour range. The silk ribbons used are a variety of plain and variegated silk ribbons. In Australia we are very lucky, because we have a large variety of Australian hand dyed ribbons. You should try as many silk ribbons as you can and then you should be the judge of which ones you like to embroider with. We all have different ideas on what we like and what we do not like. I have given you a good range of silk ribbons to try in this book and hope you like my choices.

Silk ribbons come in different widths, I have used 4mm, 7mm and 13mm wide ribbons in this book. As a designer, I am always looking for a three dimensional look to my embroidery, so I tend to use the wider silk ribbons for surface embroidery. Although, I use the wider silk ribbons mainly on the surface, I also use them through the fabric, depending on the project I am embroidering.

It is important, you only work with 12″ (30cm) of silk ribbon at any time when you are embroidering. If you use a longer length it will deteriorate. Silk ribbon is not like cotton thread, it is hardy but it must be respected and treated with some care. In some projects, I will tell you to use longer pieces of silk ribbon but these flowers are usually surface embroidered flowers.

N O T E S *on* MATERIALS *&* RIBBONS

You will notice I use unusual threads and ribbons, this is how I achieve the quality design. I do not think it is a good idea to use cheap materials if I am going to embroider a beautiful project. I was a dressmaker in my early days and I have an extensive knowledge of good quality fabrics. You might wish to substitute different fabrics for mine, but do not expect to achieve the same look. Remember, there is no substitute for quality.

If you have any trouble finding any of the requirements in this book, I am always willing to talk to you and try and help. I have my own mail order business and stock all the threads and most of the fabrics, so please call for any enquiries. I can be contacted by phone on 0412518989 or by mail at Delwood Designs, PO Box 1294, Rozelle, 2039, NSW, Australia.

N E E D L E S

The choice of needle can make or break your silk ribbon. Some silk ribbons will split when you are embroidering with them if you use the wrong size needle. I use a very large needle when I am embroidering with wider silk ribbons which have to come through the fabric. The reason for this, is the larger needle will make the hole in the fabric large enough for the silk ribbon to pass through the fabric without damaging the silk ribbon. I mainly use No 18 Chenille needles, but I have used No 14 darner needles when I have had a silk ribbon which splits. I also use the larger darner needle for wider silk ribbons which have been embroidered through the fabric. Strangely enough, some colours in the silk ribbon will split more than others. If this should occur, just use a larger needle and do not be afraid to use the darner needles. I sometimes call them crowbars, but if they work why not use them. I always use the finer Crewel needles for the fine embroidery.

STARTING & FINISHING

I never start silk ribbon embroidery with a knot in the ribbon, this is a no no as far as I am concerned. To start my silk ribbon embroidery, I have a Crewel No 9 needle threaded with a single strand of stranded thread (usually in cream colour even if I am embroidering with dark colours). This catching thread is never seen and in all of the projects in this book I recommend you use a cream thread to start and finish off.

To start your embroidery, bring the silk ribbon through to the right side of your embroidery and leave about $^1/_2$" (1cm) of silk ribbon on the back of your embroidery. Catch the small piece of silk ribbon immediately on the back of your embroidery with the Crewel needle, then end this thread off. When you have finished embroidering your flower, cut the silk ribbon leaving $^1/_2$" (1cm) hanging on the wrong side of your embroidery and then take the same needle and stranded thread you used to start with and end the silk ribbon off securely. I do not run the silk ribbon back through my embroidery as it will pull the embroidered flower tight, and if this happens you might need to embroider the flower again.

You must remember when you are embroidering with silk ribbon, it is not like embroidering with cotton or wool. While the silk ribbon is very tough it does have to be handled with some care. In this book, there are some flowers which I recommend you poke a hole in the fabric and push the end of the silk ribbon through the fabric. Make sure you start and end this silk ribbon off in the same way as I have mentioned earlier in this section. When you are embroidering Ribbon Stitch flowers, you must place a small straight stitch in the centre of each petal because the small roll at the end of the stitch in my opinion is very insecure and I think this small stitch makes the ribbon stitch more secure. Loop stitch petals are another stitch which needs to be caught in this way. You will find I secure some long straight stitches in this manner as well. Make sure you read the instructions for each project carefully.

LAUNDERING YOUR
SILK RIBBON PROJECTS

Well, as far as washing these projects, I am all for this. I do not like to have precious embroideries dry-cleaned. I am from the old school of hand washing. I wash my silk ribbon projects in cool to warm water, a wool wash. Do not let your project soak too long and the most important thing to remember is to rinse and rinse until there is no soap left in your project. The other important thing is to let your project drip dry. Try and pick the right day to wash your embroidery, do not wash it on a day when it is overcast. A fine Summer's day when the project will almost dry in one day is good, but do not worry if the embroidery takes two days to dry.

I do not iron my silk ribbon embroidery, I just hold my iron above the embroidery and let the steam bring the embroidery back to its original state. You could also give the ribbons a gentle rub with your fingers while you are steaming with your iron but make sure your hands are very clean. The other fabric around your embroidery might have to be ironed directly onto the fabric, but avoid the embroidery.

These projects are not going to be washed regularly, I can assure you. I have had my framings placed under glass to keep them clean, but I have had special staples placed on the back of the framing so the embroidery can be aired at any time. I do think the embroidery in the frame should be aired at least once or twice a year, this will stop any mould forming if your house has a dampness problem.

PREPARING *to* START YOUR SILK RIBBON EMBROIDERY

You must always hand tack the cotton voile to the wrong side of the fabric to be used. The hand tacking is approx. $^1/2''$ (1 cm) in from the raw edge. It is a good idea to overlock or oversew the raw edges to avoid fraying while you are embroidering.

The next important thing to remember when you are embroidering with silk ribbon is you must always embroider in a hoop. The fine embroidery can be embroidered out of the hoop, but the silk ribbon embroidery must be done in a hoop. I like to use a spring hoop because if I have to move the hoop, and it goes over my previously embroidered work, it does not damage the silk ribbon. I find a wooden hoop, even if it has the bottom hoop bound, will still damage the silk ribbon. You might find it difficult to embroider in a hoop at first, but if you do not use a hoop your tension will be incorrect. A spring hoop does not hold the fabric drum tight and this will help you to conquer the use of a hoop.

Silk ribbon is embroidered using a loose tension. It is never pulled tight. In all my embroidery, I am always looking for a three dimensional look. I do not use a hoop for the fine embroidery, as I find I cannot embroider my leaves etc. small enough. If you are comfortable using a hoop for fine embroidery, go ahead and use it. If you are stitching straight stitches in a silk ribbon embroidered flower, I find you get a better result using a hoop. Should you be embroidering a flower like the Waratah, which has a large amount of colonial knots, I find a hoop an advantage. I usually use a 7″ or 5″ (18cm or 13cm) spring hoop.

TRANSFERRING INSTRUCTIONS

To transfer the design to your fabric is quite simple. Take a piece of tracing paper the size of the graph and mark the centre of each flower with a dot, or mark the entire flower if you want. I use pencil to mark the design on the tracing paper only. Now with a needle, poke a hole where you have made the dots and place the tracing paper onto the fabric. It is a good idea if you have a large design to hand tack the tracing paper onto the fabric, but with a small design you can use pins to hold it in place.

Take your water soluble pen, and through the holes, press the markings firmly onto the fabric. You will end up with a series of dots and these represent your flowers. Mark each section in this manner and only mark a small section at a time. I do not like to use pencil to transfer my designs, I prefer to use a water soluble pen and I wet it well to remove the blue markings once I have completed my embroidery.

Remember, if you embroider smaller than I do, you might need to add extra flowers to your design. If you embroider larger than I do, you might need to leave some flowers out. My designs are only a guide, as we all have different tensions.

N O T E *o n* D O L L S

The half dolls used in this book have been especially painted to match my embroidery. Small handmade roses have also been added to enhance the dolls. I used to paint dolls so I know what I am looking for when I design these dolls. I am quite happy to help you regarding these dolls. I can be contacted by phone on 0412518989 or by mail at Delwood Designs, PO Box 1294, Rozelle, 2039, NSW, Australia.

Running Stitch

Run the needle along the fabric, making small stitches of equal length and picking up an equal amount of fabric between each stitch.

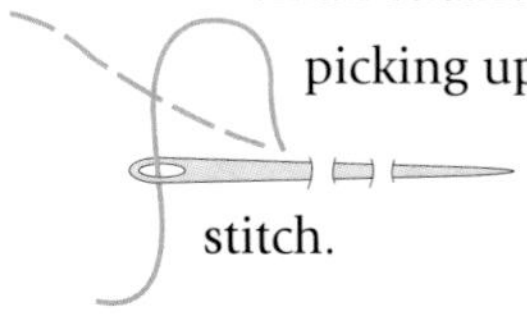

you. Do not wind the thread too tight. The number of twists depends on the flower you are embroidering. When you have the required amount of twists on the needle, hold the twists gently and pull the needle through them.

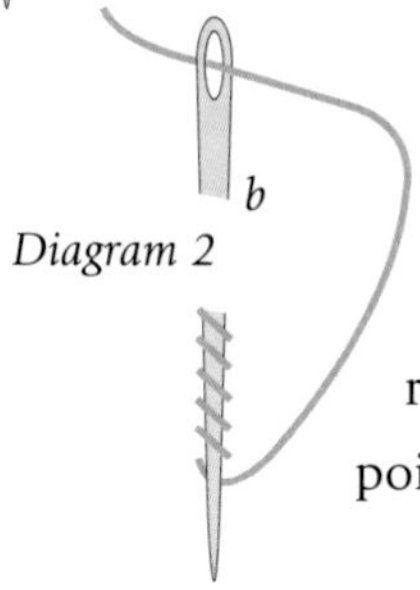

Make sure the twists are evenly spaced down the thread. Reinsert the needle and thread at B, and pull through the fabric.

Straight Stitch

Bring the needle up at A and take it down at B. Be careful not to pull the thread too tight.

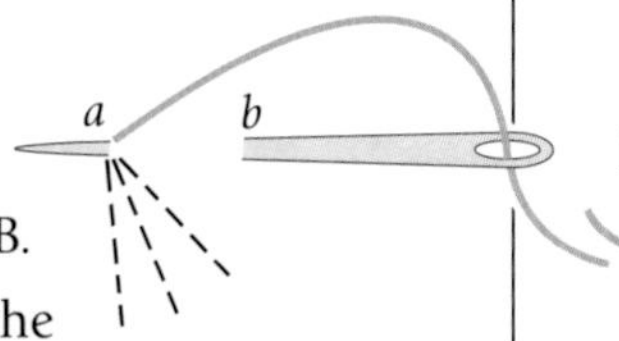

a   *b*

Bullion Stitch

Bring the needle and thread up through the fabric at A and insert the needle at B. The distance between A and B will vary according to the flower being embroidered.

Bring the needle up again at A. Pull the needle part of the way through the fabric, but do not bring the eye of the needle through.

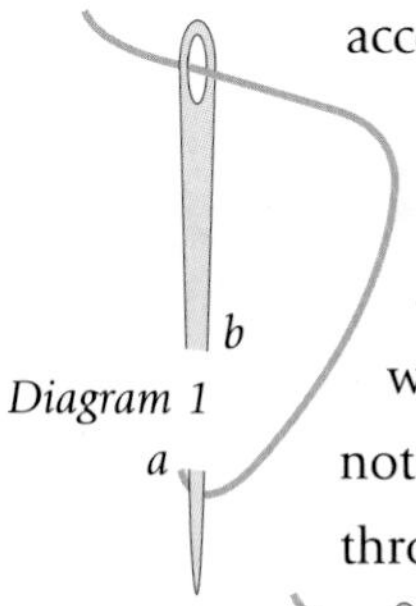

Diagram 1

b

a

Start winding the thread around the point of the needle (clockwise if you are right handed) with the point of the needle facing

Diagram 2

b

Buttonhole Stitch

Mark the centre point, A, and bring the needle up through the fabric at B. Insert the needle at A and come out again with the thread below the needle beside B. Pull the needle out to form the stitch.

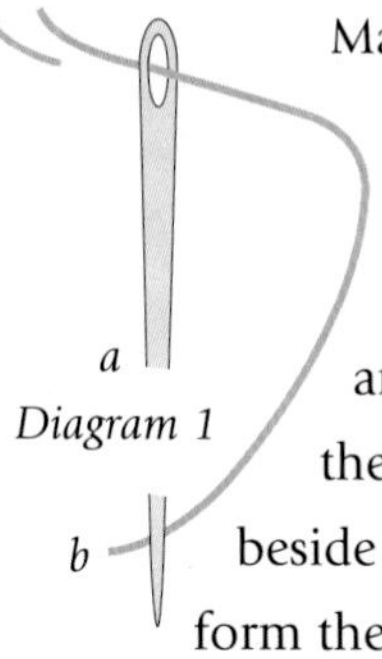

a

Diagram 1

b

Continue in this manner, working from left to right. Insert the needle at A all the time, but move around at B to form a circle or half-circle, depending on which flower you are working.

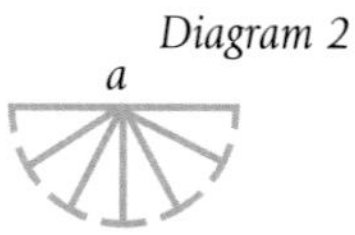

Diagram 2

a

Chain Stitch

Bring the needle up at A. Make a loop with the thread on the surface of the fabric, and hold it in place with your left thumb.

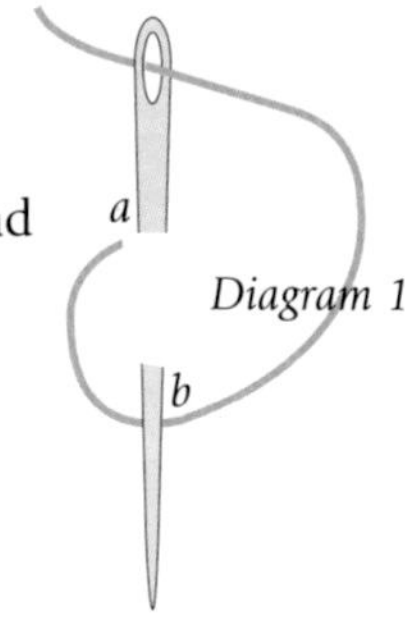

a

Diagram 1

b

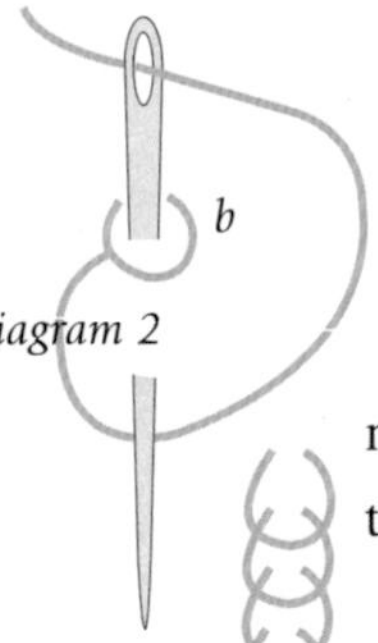

Diagram 2

Insert the needle again at A and bring the needle out at B. Keep the thread under the point of the needle, thus maintaining the loop. Pull the thread, but not tightly.

Repeat this process again, only this time come up at B.

Diagram 3

When you have completed the required number of chain stitches, end the last stitch with a stitch over the loop.

Whipped Chain Stitch

Embroider the chain stitch first following instructions for chain stitch.

Bring the needle up through the fabric at A. Leading with the eye of the needle, slide the needle under the chain stitch, but do not go through the fabric. Pull the thread, but not tightly.

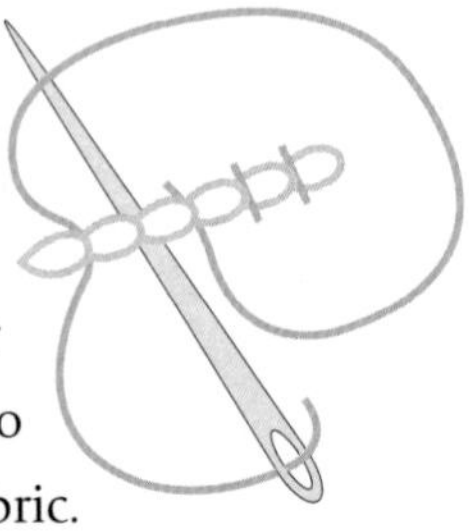

Continue sliding the needle and thread under each chain stitch until you reach the end. Take the thread through to the back of the fabric, and end off.

It is important when whipping that the thread is long enough to whip the entire section, as you cannot join the thread once you have started.

Ribbon Stitch

Bring the needle up at A and lay the ribbon flat on the fabric.

Place the point of the needle into the centre of the ribbon at B.

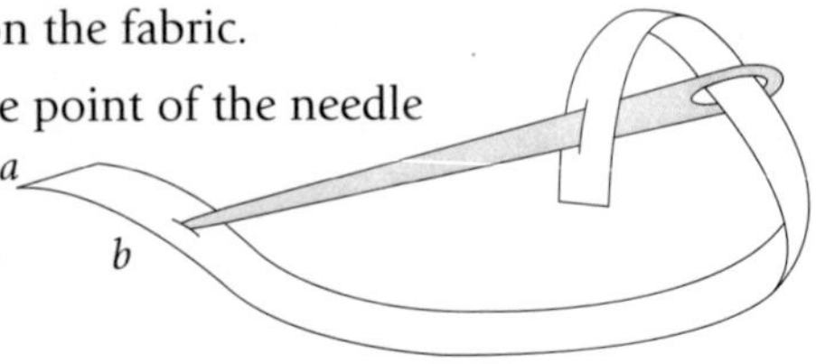

Pull the ribbon through the fabric, but be careful not to pull the ribbon too tight. The edges of the ribbon will slightly curl over.

Threading the Needle for Silk Ribbon

To thread the needle (usually a No 18 Chenille, but please check your instructions) pass the end of the silk ribbon through the eye of the needle. Then place the point of the needle through the end of the ribbon, about $1/4''$ (4mm) from the end of the ribbon. Pull firmly on the ribbon so it is right up at the eye of the needle.

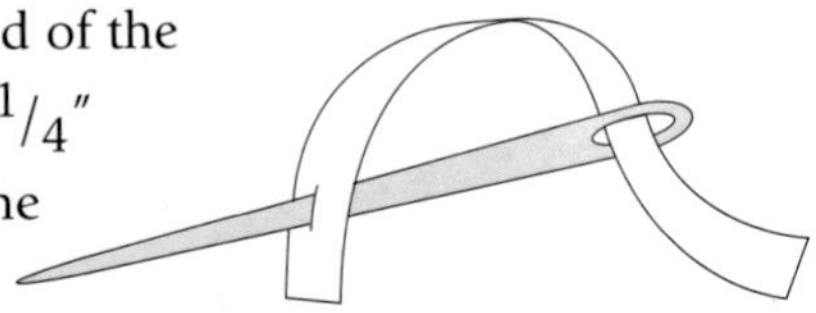

By following this method of threading, you will use all of your ribbon when stitching.

Starting Your Silk Ribbon

When using silk ribbon, you do not tie knots. In most of the projects I have listed a Cream stranded thread, either Ecru or No 712. You must use two strands in a No 9 Crewel needle to anchor your silk ribbon at the back of your embroidery. When starting your silk ribbon, bring the ribbon through to the right side of your embroidery but leave $1/2$" (1cm) of ribbon hanging at the back of your work. Secure the end of the ribbon with the stranded thread needle and then end off this thread (or it might get in the way as you start to embroider). The ribbon is now secure to start your embroidery.

Ending Off Your Silk Ribbon

Cut the silk ribbon off when you have finished embroidering, leaving $1/2$" (1cm) hanging. Using the same thread you started off with (No 9 Crewel needle with two strands of stranded thread), secure the end of the silk ribbon off with a couple of overstitches.

Lazy Daisy Stitch

Bring the needle up through the fabric at the inside of the petal, at A. Insert the needle back at B and bring it up again just outside the tip of the petal, at C. The length of the petal will depend on the type of flower you are embroidering.

Loop the thread around the needle and pull the needle and thread through the fabric.

Anchor the loop with a tiny straight stitch at the tip of the

petal. This stitch can vary in length according to the flower you are embroidering.

When you are embroidering a five petal flower, it is easier to embroider the first three petals in the shape of a letter Y and then embroider two petals in-between. This method will always give you five even petals.

Fly Stitch

Fly stitch can be used for flowers, leaves and trimming on other flowers.

When embroidering fly stitch, you must always start from the outside and work in, especially with continuous fly stitch.

Bring the needle up through the fabric at A. Then insert the needle the required distance to the right of A, at B. Bring the needle out halfway between A and B, at C.

Anchor the loop with a straight stitch, taking the needle to the back of the work at D. The length of the stitch can vary according to the flower or leaves you are working.

Continuous Fly Stitch

To work continuous fly stitch, follow the instructions for fly stitch, but instead of finishing off each stitch join on another stitch. In some designs when using continuous fly stitch you might have to start with a straight stitch first, check your design.

Feather Stitch

Feather stitch is one stitch to the left and one stitch to the right of the line to be covered. The stitch itself is like a fly stitch, without the anchoring stitch. When embroidering this stitch you must always start from the outside and work in.

Bring the needle up at A, then across the line to the right and into the fabric at B. Come out of the fabric again at C, looping the thread under the needle as in fly stitch.

Repeat the same stitch, this time to the left of the line.

Satin Stitch

Satin stitches are straight stitches worked side by side. Work them close together to cover the fabric well.

Bring the needle up at A and take it down at B. Use a stabbing motion for better tension.

Work the second stitch, from C to D, as close to the first stitch as possible. Continue in this same manner until you have covered the area being stitched.

Ladder Stitch

Ladder stitch is used to close openings. It is basically a small running stitch.

Take one tiny stitch on the seam line of the top opening and take one stitch on the seam line of the bottom opening. Pull the thread firmly. The raw edges will turn inside.

Stem Stitch

Work this stitch from left to right with small stitches all the same length.

Bring the needle up at A and take it down at B.

Then bring it up at C, just above the previous stitch, making sure the thread is always on the bottom of the needle.

Colonial Knot

Bring the needle up through the fabric at A.

Place your left hand under the thread, and pass the needle under the thread, from left to right, Diagram 1.

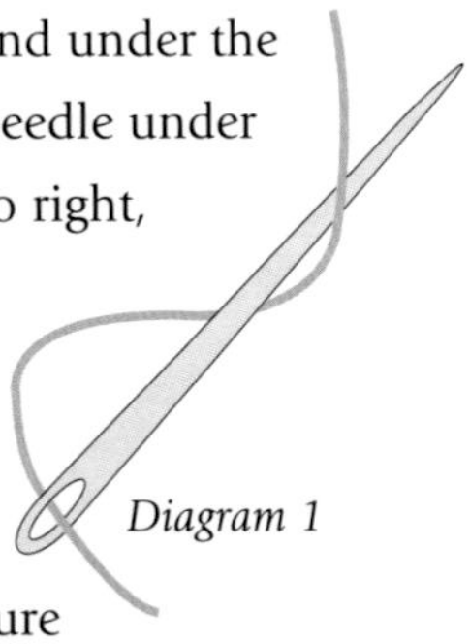

a

Now lift the thread up and over the needle from left to right, forming a figure of eight, Diagram 2.

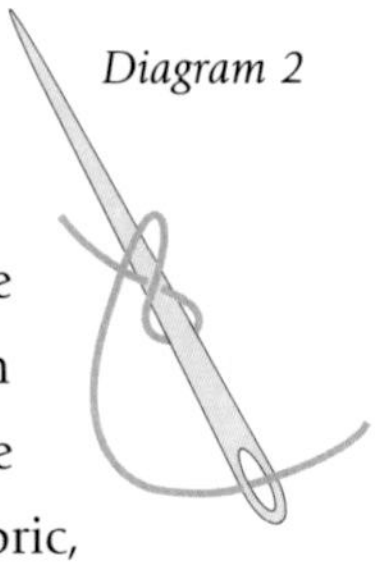

Diagram 1

Diagram 2

Insert the needle into the fabric very near to where the thread first came up and pull the knot down the needle. Pull the needle and thread through the fabric, making sure you hold the knot as you pull through. If you find the knot has gone to the wrong side, then you have gone back through the same hole as you came up.

Stem Rose Stitch

An important point to remember with these roses is, they need to be embroidered very small. I would suggest you have a practice run on a scrap of fabric before you start these projects.

Draw a very small circle (no larger than the smaller circle shown in Diagram 1) with a water soluble pen. This marks the outer edge of the rose.

Diagram 1

Using a double or single strand of the required thread, start with a knot and a backstitch to secure the knot. Work in stem stitch, but keep the stitches very loose. You will have a loop on the right side of your work. Embroider stem stitches around the circle in an anti-clockwise direction until it is full, Diagram 2.

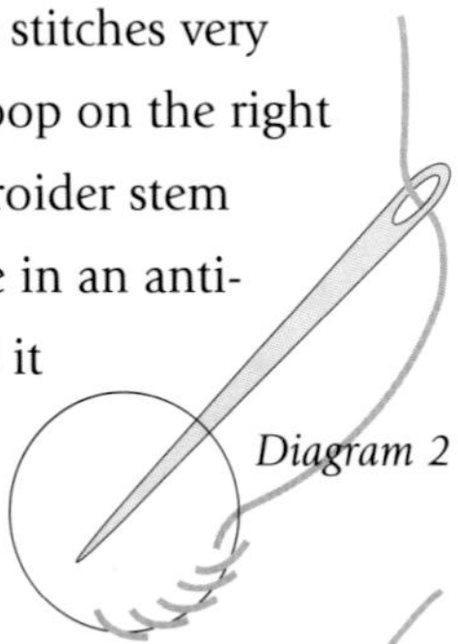

Diagram 2

Even though it might seem impossible, you will be able to fit another small row of stem stitches inside the outer circle, Diagram 3. You might only fit three stem stitches in this row.

Diagram 3

To finish off the flowers, take the thread down through the centre of the rose, leaving the loop loose. Finish the thread off at the back of the work, being careful not to pull the loop tight.

Carnations/Roses

Check your project instructions for the amount of silk ribbon needed for each Carnation. Sometimes these flowers are called Carnations, at other times they are referred to as Roses. Please read the instructions carefully.

Fold over the ends of the ribbon.

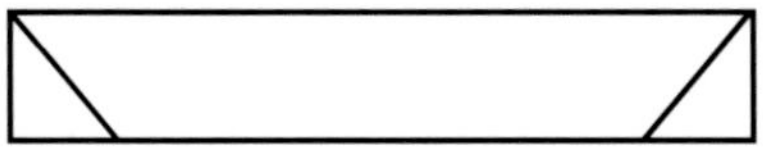

With one strand of stranded thread and a Crewel No 9 needle,

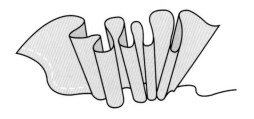

work a running stitch along the bottom edge of the ribbon, but do not end off as you will gather the ribbon in with this thread.

Gather the ribbon in before you start to sew the Carnation onto the fabric.

This flower is stitched from the centre and then worked outwards. Take another strand of stranded thread and secure this to the centre of the Carnation. Start to sew the ribbon onto the fabric, in a snail like direction (you will be sewing in an anti-clockwise direction). The stitches must be very small.

When you have completed sewing all the ribbon around, end the sewing thread off securely. Re-thread your gathering thread and take it through to the wrong side of the fabric and end this thread off. You have now completed your Carnation.

Chrysanthemum
Step 1

Take your piece of cotton voile, or whatever your project suggests, and place the fabric into your hoop.

Draw a circle the size of your diagram using a water soluble pen.

Fill the circle with colonial knots, using the thread suggested in your instructions. Embroider the colonial knots very close together, using six strands (in some projects you might use only three strands). Check your project instructions for the number of strands to use.

In some projects you will add a few glass seed beads to the colonial knots (the colours will be in your instructions). To hand sew the seed beads on you should use two strands of stranded cotton and a Crewel No 10 needle. When threading two strands of stranded thread, it is best to cut your thread a little longer and thread one strand through the eye of the needle, taking the thread down to form two threads. Tie the two ends together in a knot. By using this method you will have less bulk going through the eye of the needle and the glass seed bead.

Step 2

Cut the circle of knots out along the dotted line. Using a matching thread to the  knots, hand sew the excess fabric into the centre of the circle on the back of the fabric. When all the fabric is sewn in place, position the circle where marked on your design and begin to hand sew the

centre in place using the same thread used to sew the excess fabric to the back of the circle. The circle of knots is sewn on using a stab stitch. Stab stitching is just small straight stitches coming up and going back down through the fabric. These stitches must be very small because we want the raised centre to sit flat. You do not want to see any of the folded in fabric. It is a good idea to embroider this step in a hoop.

Step 3

Take 18″ (45cm) of 7mm wide silk ribbon (or the amount and width mentioned in your project). Run a small

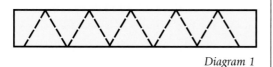

Diagram 1

running stitch (in a wave motion as per Diagram 1) along the length of your ribbon. Make sure you secure your thread very carefully at the start, which is $^1/_2$″ (1cm) in from the raw end of the ribbon. Stop $^1/_2$″ (1cm) from the end, but do not end this thread off.

Gather the silk ribbon in to fit around the circle of colonial knots comfortably, again do not end this thread off.

Using a stiletto, poke a hole in your fabric and push the starting end of the silk ribbon through the hole. Secure the end of the silk ribbon at the

back of your work using two strands of stranded thread and a No 9 Crewel needle. Poke the other end of the ribbon through the fabric in the same manner, very close to where you pushed the starting end through and secure in place as before. Gather the ribbon in now to fit snugly around the circle of knots. Now using the same coloured thread as your ribbon, hand sew the ruched ribbon around the circle of knots. Use a stab stitch through the centre of the gathered ribbon, making sure the stitches are very small (so you do not see them on the right side of the ribbon). Sewing the ribbon on is best done in a hoop.

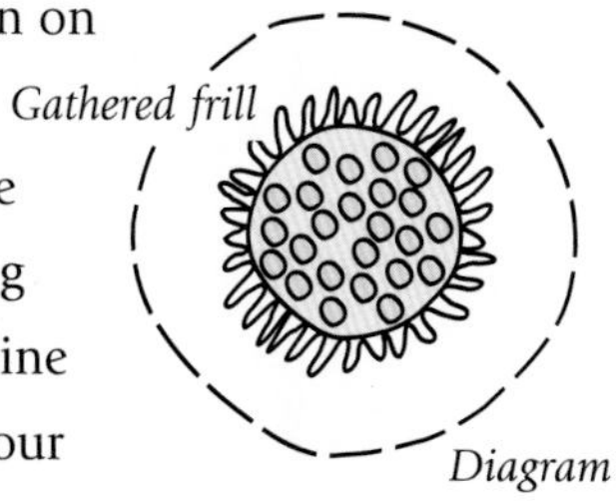

Draw a circle, the same size as the Diagram 2, using a water soluble pen. This line will make it easy to keep your petals even. Embroider the petals where marked on Diagram 3, each petal is one ribbon stitch. This will ensure your petals are evenly placed around the circle.

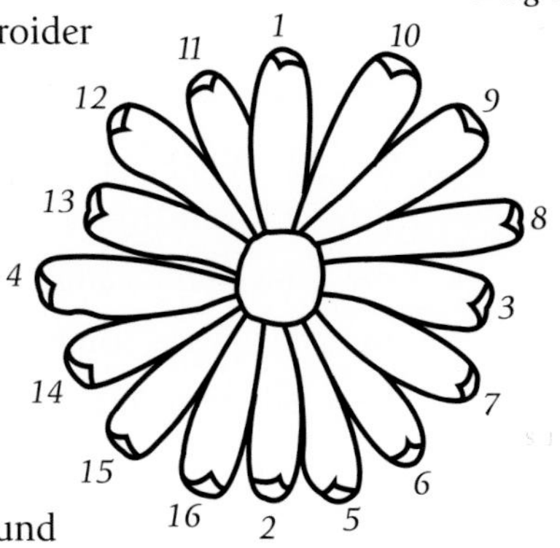

Gathered frill

Diagram 2

Diagram 3

It is a good idea to stitch a small straight stitch in the centre of each petal, using one strand of matching thread, at the base of each petal. Use a No 9 Crewel

29

needle for this stitch. If you work this straight stitch as you embroider each silk ribbon petal, you will be less likely to pull your ribbon stitch through. These petals should also be embroidered in a hoop.

Centres for Flannel Flowers, Everlasting Daisies and the white Daisies in the daisy arrangement

These are embroidered the same as the centres for the Chrysanthemums, but in the Flannel Flowers and small

Diagram 1
Diagram 2

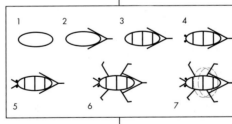

Everlasting Daisies the centres are smaller, Diagram 1. The centres for the white Daisies (in the framing) are slightly larger, Diagram 2.

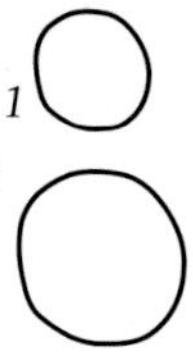

Check your project instructions to see how many strands, which colours and whether to use any seed beads.

The Large Bee

Please read your project instructions to see what colours and threads to use. Some bees will have gold stripes and some will have black stripes.

Step 1

Embroider the bee's body in satin stitch, in the thread mentioned in your instructions, Diagram 1.

Step 2

Embroider the bee's body stripes and sting, using either one strand of gold thread or six strands of black stranded thread. Please check your instructions for threads.

Step 3

The sting is embroidered first. The sting is one fly stitch at the back of the bee's body with the holding stitch extended a little to form the sting, Diagram 2.

Step 4

The stripes on the bee's body are embroidered, using the same thread as the sting. The stripes are straight stitches across the bee's body. It is best to embroider the back stripe from the fly stitch first and then embroider the front stripe next. Finally, embroider one stripe in the middle of these stripes, Diagram 3.

Step 5

Embroider the bee's eyes, using the same thread as the stripes. Each eye is one colonial knot and the knots are very close together, Diagram 4. Check the instructions in your project to see how many threads you should use.

Embroider the feelers next. The feelers are two straight stitches in the

shape of a V, between the eyes. It is best if you start your straight stitches from the outside and go between the eyes, Diagram 5.

Step 6

Embroider the bee's legs, using the same thread as the eyes. Check your instructions for colours and the number of strands. The legs are four long straight stitches, with four shorter straight stitches for the bend in the bee's leg, Diagram 6.

Step 7

Embroider the bee's wings, using bullion stitch and the thread mentioned in your instructions. Each bee has two wings on each side of its body. Each wing is a bullion stitch using twenty-five twists. I usually use a No 18 Chenille needle if I am using DMC Perle thread, Diagram 7.

The Small Bee

Step 1

This bee is very different to the larger bee.

Embroider the bee's body, using two strands of stranded thread (usually yellow). Check your instructions for colours. The body is five or seven very small satin stitches. Embroider the bee's sting next, using two strands of black stranded thread. Embroider one very small fly stitch at the back of the bee's

body, extending the holding stitch a little longer to form the sting, Diagram 1.

Step 2

Embroider the front stripe and one stripe over the fly stitch at the back of the bee's body. These stripes are small straight stitches (usually two strands of black stranded thread, but check your

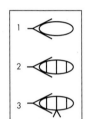

instructions). Embroider one stripe in the middle of the front and back stripe using the same thread, Diagram 2.

Step 3

Embroider two small straight stitches in the shape of a V, using one strand of the same thread as the stripes, to form the bee's legs, Diagram 3.

Step 4

Embroider the bee's eyes, using one strand of the same thread as the legs. Each eye is one colonial knot and the two eyes must be very close together. Embroider the feelers next, using one strand of the same thread. The feelers are two very small straight stitches in the shape of a V. It is best if you embroider the feelers from the outside in between the eyes, Diagram 4.

Step 5

Embroider the bee's wings, using a single strand of black and gold thread (check your instructions for the correct colour and thread). The bee has two wings on the top of its body. Each wing is one small lazy daisy stitch with the holding stitch extended slightly longer, Diagram 5.

Waratah Flower

Step 1

Draw the top of the Waratah from Diagram 1. Fill this shape with colonial knots, using six strands of stranded thread DMC No 75, variegated reds. The colonial knots must be packed in very tight and you should not see any of the linen fabric through the knots. I use a No18 Chenille needle for the knots. It is not a good idea to embroider the colonial knots in rows as the effect will look too regimented. It is best if you work all over the shape and have no lines. I think the shape appears to fill up quicker if you use this method.

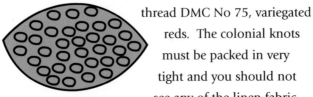

Diagram 1

Step 2

Take $19^1/_2$ " (50cm) of 13mm wide silk ribbon No 2 – 1315 variegated reds. Thread a No 9 Crewel needle with one strand of stranded thread No 75. You are going to embroider a small wave like running stitch along the length of the

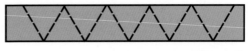

Diagram 2

ribbon. Make sure you start and finish $1/_2$ " (1cm) in from the end of the ribbon. Start with a knot and an overstitch but stop $1/_2$ " (1cm) from the end. Do not end this thread off, Diagram 2.

Step 3

Poke a hole with the stiletto at the top left hand side of the Waratah. Push the ribbon through the hole and secure at the back of your work with another single thread, the same colour as the red ribbon. Poke another hole at the right hand side of the top of the Waratah and repeat the same step as the first side. Now gather the ribbon in, using the wave thread. The ribbon must sit comfortably around the lower edge of the Waratah. Now secure the wave thread, but do not cut it off. Using this same thread, stab stitch through the centre of the gathered ribbon to attach the frill of the Waratah. These stab stitches must be very small and not seen on the right side of the ribbon, Diagram 3.

Diagram 3

Step 4

The leaves of the Waratah flower are medium size back stitches, using 4mm wide silk ribbon. The vein of the leaf is continuous fly stitch using the colour mentioned in your project. Make sure you start the vein from the top of the leaf and work down. Start the vein off with a straight stitch and then continuous fly stitch, Diagram 4.

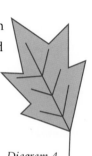

Diagram 4

Loop Stitch

Bring your needle up at A and take it down again at B. B is quite close to A at its back, Diagram 1. Do not pull the ribbon tight, thus forming a loop on the top of your embroidery. Each loop is approx $^3/_8$" (7mm) in length. Catch each loop with a small straight stitch, in the centre of the ribbon, at the base of the loop stitch. This stitch is usually a small straight stitch, enough to stop the loop being pulled through the fabric when you are embroidering your next loop stitch. Use one strand of matching thread and a No 9 Crewel needle.

a   b

Loop stitch

Loop Stitch Flowers

Draw a small circle with a water soluble pen, Diagram 1. Embroider eight or nine loop stitch petals around your circle, catching each petal as you go. Do not make the loops too large, the loop stitch measurement is quite a good size. I find 12" (30cm) of silk ribbon is sufficient to make a nice flower. It will depend on how big you draw the centre circle. When you have completed your circle of loop stitches, secure the ribbon off. If you have secured each petal as you embroidered, you can now fill the centre of the loop stitch flower with beads or colonial knots, please check your project for instructions. If your instructions are to fill the centre with glass seed beads, fill the centre with beads using a No.10 Crewel needle and two strands of matching thread (until the whole centre is full). I usually pile some beads on top of each other to get the centre to raise up, Diagram 2.

Diagram 1

Diagram 2

Side Ribbon Stitch

This stitch is the same as the normal ribbon stitch, but instead of placing the needle in the centre of the ribbon come up at the side edge of the ribbon. Sometimes you will take the stitch to the right of the ribbon and other times you will go the left of the ribbon.

Use your own judgement when embroidering the leaves up the stem regarding which side you take the side ribbon stitch to. Diagram 1 is on one edge and Diagram 2 is on the other edge.

Diagram 1

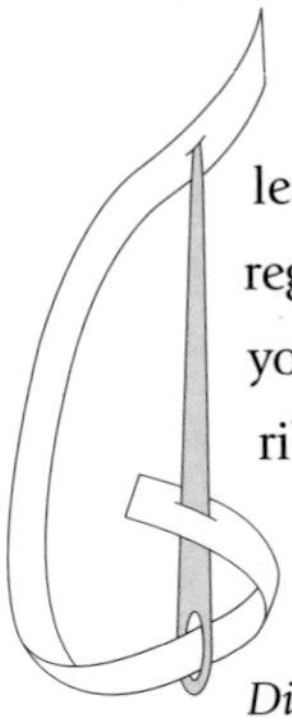

Diagram 2

The Sturt's Desert Pea Flower
Step 1

Embroider the centre of the pea first using the ribbon mentioned in your project and approx ten colonial knots, in two rows, Diagram 1.

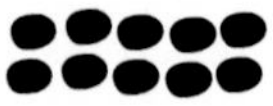

Diagram 1

Step 2

Embroider the pea's petals, using the recommended ribbon. Embroider the centre petal on the bottom of the pea flower first, using large lazy daisy stitches. This petal is slightly larger than the two petals either side of it. Extend the holding stitch a little longer and embroider one straight stitch in the centre of each petal, using the same ribbon. Embroider one lazy daisy stitch petal either side of the centre petal, using the same ribbon, extending the holding stitch

Diagram 2

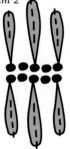

a little longer. The petals on either side of the centre petal are not as long. Repeat this step for the top petals of the pea flower, Diagram 2.

Step 3

Embroider the stem, using the recommended thread and stem stitch. The leaves are one fly stitch with a straight stitch in the centre, using the ribbon recommended in your project, Diagram 3.

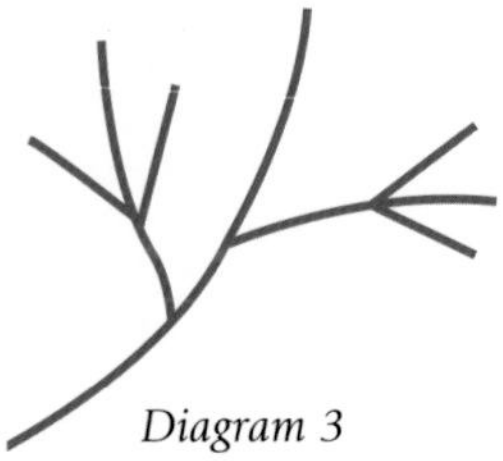

Diagram 3

The Bottle Brush Flower
Step 1

Embroider the centre colonial knots, using the recommended ribbon.

Each flower will have seven or eight knots. These knots are quite close together. Embroider five straight stitches at the end of the flower using the same ribbon, Diagram 1.

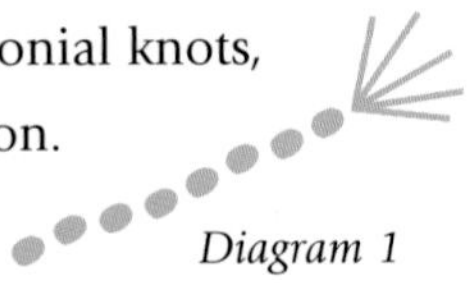

Diagram 1

Step 2

Embroider the petals of the flower, using the recommended ribbon. Each petal is one straight stitch. I embroidered each alternate petal a little longer than the previous petal, Diagram 2.

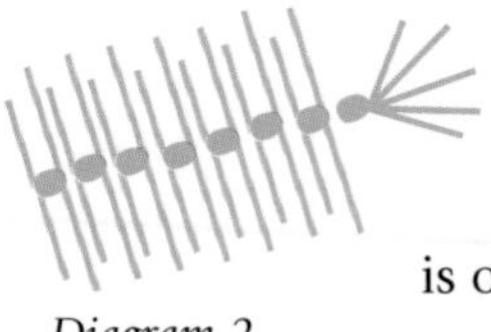

Diagram 2

Step 3

Embroider one colonial knot on the end of each petal, using the thread mentioned in your project, Diagram 3.

Diagram 3

Step 4

Embroider the stems of the Bottle Brush, using the recommended colour and stem stitch. If you start your stem stitch from the bottom up, then all the stems will be in the same direction. Embroider the leaves using side ribbon stitch, Diagram 4.

Diagram 4

The Flannel Flower

Step 1

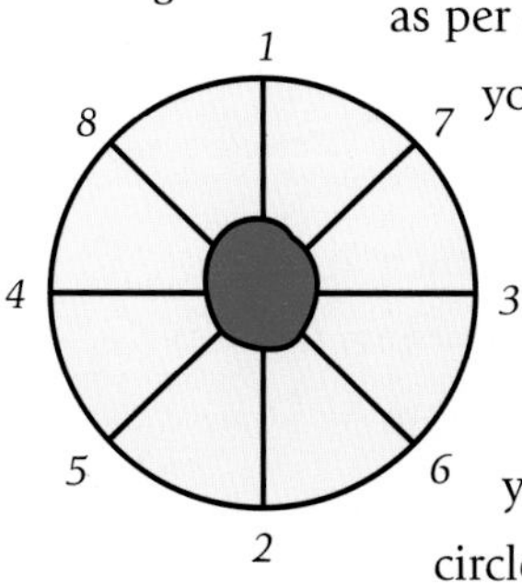

Make the centre of the Flannel Flower as per separate instructions. Check your project for colours.

Diagram 1

Step 2

Draw a circle the size of the Flannel Flower with your water soluble pen. This circle will make sure all your petals are the same length. Each petal is one straight stitch, using the recommended ribbon. Do not pull the stitches tight. Embroider the petals as per Diagram 1. Embroider one small straight stitch in the centre of the petal, at the base of the petal, using a No 9 Crewel needle

and one strand of matching stranded thread, Diagram 2.

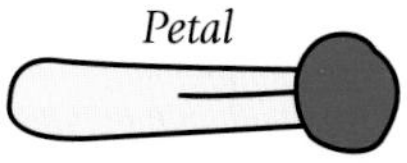

Petal

Diagram 2

Step 3

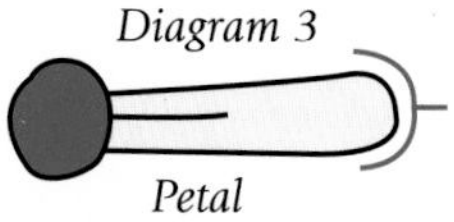

Embroider the greenery around the end of each petal, using the recommended colours. Embroider one fly stitch, half way up each petal and extend the holding stitch a little longer, Diagram 3.

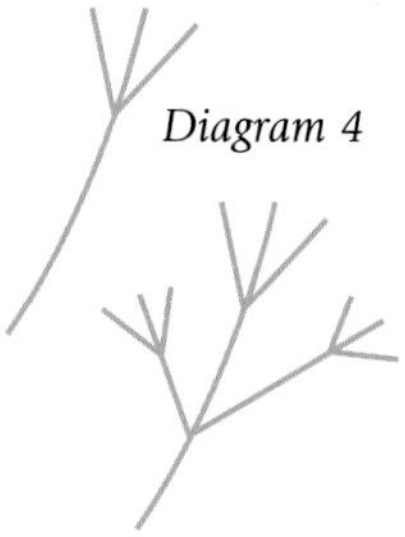

Diagram 3

Petal

Step 4

Embroider the stems and leaves, using the recommended colours. Embroider one straight stitch to start your stems off, starting from the outside. Then embroider one fly stitch and medium back stitch for the remaining stem. Embroider other leaves out from the joins of the back stitch, using one straight stitch and then one fly stitch, Diagram 4.

Diagram 4

The Everlasting Daisies

Step 1

Embroider the centres of the Daisies as per separate instructions. Check your project for colours.

Step 2

Embroider the petals, using the recommended ribbon. Each petal is one straight stitch, not too tight. It is a good

Diagram 1

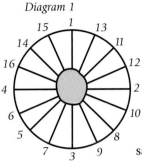

idea to draw a circle the size of the Daisy, with the water soluble pen. If you follow this step, all your petals will end up the same length, Diagram 1.

Step 3

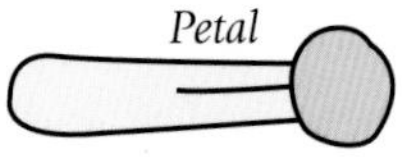

Petal

Diagram 2

Embroider one very small straight stitch in the centre of each petal, at the base of the petal, using a No 9 Crewel needle and one strand of matching thread, Diagram 2.

Step 4

Embroider the Daisy stems, using the recommended colours and stem stitch. Embroider all stems in the same direction. The leaves are slightly loose straight stitches embroidered up the stem.

The Tea Tree Flower

Step 1

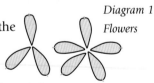

Diagram 1

Flowers

Embroider the flowers, using five even lazy daisy stitch petals and the recommended ribbon, Diagram 1. Embroider the buds, using the same ribbon. Each bud is one lazy daisy stitch, Diagram 2.

Diagram 2

Buds

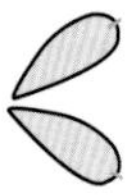

Step 2

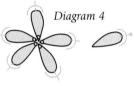

Diagram 3

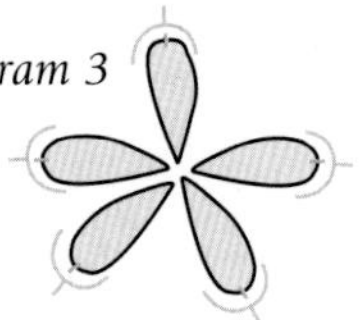

Embroider the fly stitch around the outer edge of each petal and bud, using the recommended thread. Each petal has a fly stitch half way up, with the holding stitch extended a little longer, Diagram 3.

Step 3

Embroider the centres of the flowers, using the recommended colours. The centres are four colonial knots, using two colours blended. Work an additional colonial knot on the end of each bud, using the same threads, Diagram 4.

Diagram 4

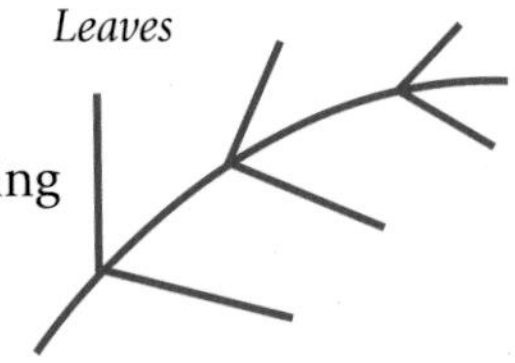

Step 4

Diagram 5

Leaves

Embroider the leaves, using the recommended colours. The leaves are continuous fly stitch. Start with a straight stitch at the outer edge and then work continuous fly stitch down to the flowers, Diagram 5.

The Royal Blue Bell Flower

Step 1

Diagram 1

Diagram 2

Embroider the flowers, using the recommended ribbon. Each flower has five evenly placed petals, using a lazy daisy stitch for each petal, Diagram 1. Each bud is one lazy daisy stitch, Diagram 2.

Step 2

Using the recommended thread, tip each petal and bud with a fly stitch and extend the holding stitch a little longer, Diagram 3.

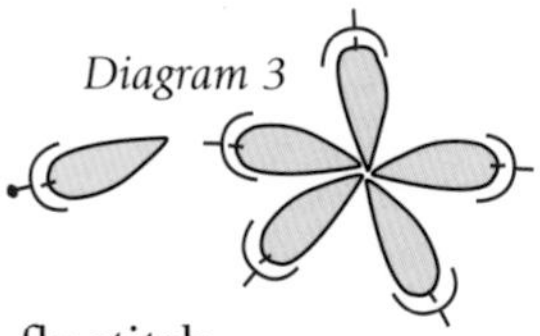

Diagram 3

Step 3

Embroider the leaves, using the recommended thread. Each leaf is one lazy daisy stitch, Diagram 4. Embroider the greenery around the buds next, using the recommended thread. Embroider one fly stitch around the bud, but do not extend the holding stitch. Embroider another fly stitch around the first fly stitch, extending the holding stitch back to the flowers to form the stem of the bud, Diagram 5.

Diagram 4

Diagram 5

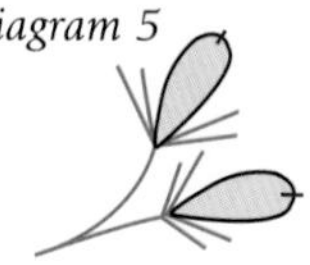

Step 4

Embroider the centre of the flower, using six strands of the recommended stranded thread. The centre is one pistil stitch, Diagram 6.

Diagram 6

The Lemon Gum Blossom Flower

Step 1

Embroider the stems of the blossom, using the recommended thread and stem stitch. Make sure you embroider all the stems in the same direction. Work the pod next, using the recommended thread. Each pod is a half circle of closely worked buttonhole stitches, Diagram 1.

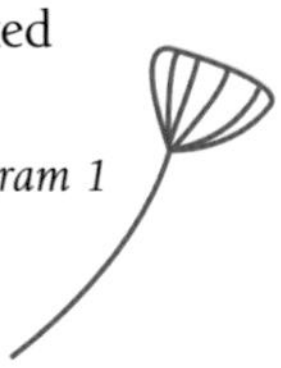

Diagram 1

Step 2

Embroider the petals of the blossom, using the recommended ribbon. The petals are small straight stitches very close together. Embroider the first row all the same length, but leave enough space in between each petal to fit the next row of petals, Diagram 2. Embroider the second row of petals the same length as the first row, but embroider this row in between the first row starting half way down. The petals will look longer because you have started half way down, Diagram 3. Embroider a colonial knot on the end of each petal, using the recommended thread, Diagram 4.

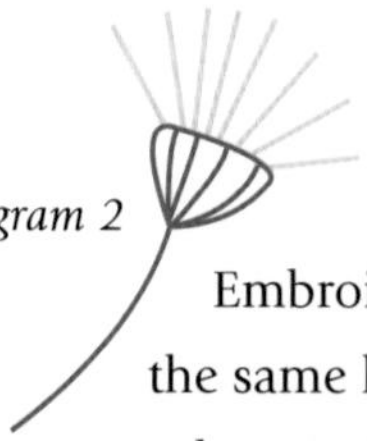

Diagram 2

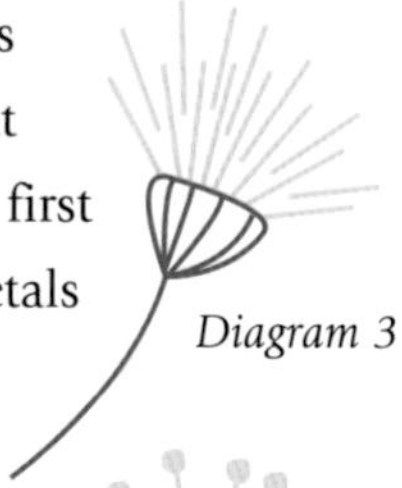

Diagram 3

Diagram 4

Step 3

Embroider the blossom leaf, using the ribbon mentioned in your project. The leaves are one long side ribbon stitch, Diagram 5. It is a good idea to embroider one small straight stitch in the centre of the leaf, at the base of the leaf, using one strand of matching stranded thread.

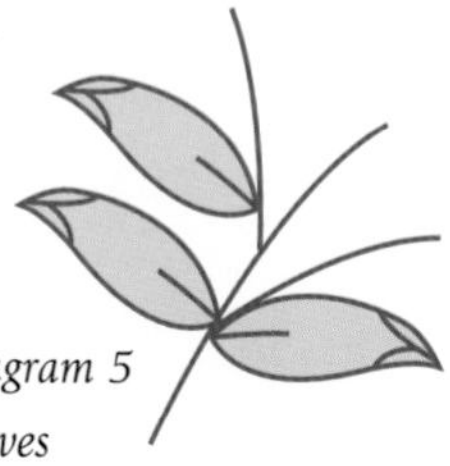

Diagram 5
Leaves

The Pink Gum Flower

Embroider the pink blossom following the same instructions as for the lemon blossom, but change the colours according to your project instructions.

The Lady Bird

Embroider the lady beetles legs, using two strands of stranded thread No 310 black. Embroider six small straight stitches for each leg, Diagram 1 and one smaller straight stitch for the bend of each leg, Diagram 2.

Securely sew on the lady beetle button in the centre of the legs.

Diagram 1

Diagram 2

The Wattle Flower

Step 1

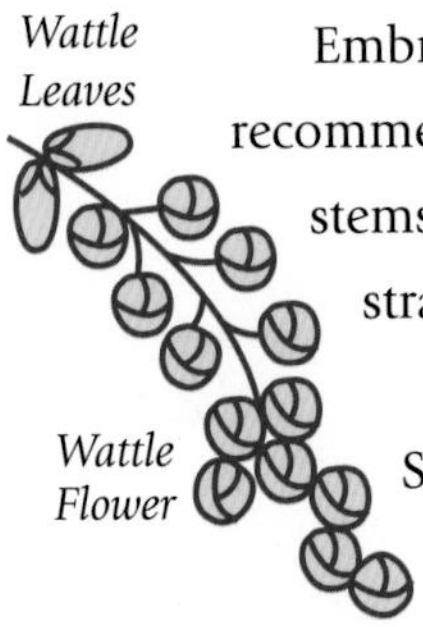

Embroider the stems, using the recommended stranded thread. The stems are stem stitch, using two strands of stranded thread.

Wattle Leaves

Wattle Flower

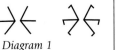

Step 2

Embroider the Wattle blossom, using the recommended ribbon. Each flower is one very loose colonial knot, using 7mm wide silk ribbon. When you wind the silk ribbon around the needle, make sure the ribbon is very loose. Also remember, when you pull the ribbon through the fabric, do not pull the ribbon tight (as you usually do) before you pull the needle through the fabric.

Step 3

Embroider the Wattle leaves, using the recommended ribbon Each leaf is one ribbon stitch. Embroider one small straight stitch in the centre of each leaf, using one strand of matching stranded thread and a No 9 Crewel needle.

The Wheat Ears

Step 1

Embroider the centre stem of the wheat, using stem stitch and two strands of the recommended stranded thread.

Step 2

Embroider the ears of the wheat, using three strands of the recommended stranded thread. Each wheat ear is one lazy daisy stitch with the holding stitch extended a little longer. Embroider one straight stitch in each lazy daisy stitch, using the same thread, Diagrams 1 & 2.

Diagram 1

Diagram 2

Step 3

Embroider one straight stitch in between each wheat ear, using the recommended Perle thread. This stitch is longer than the wheat ear, Diagram 3.

Diagram 3

The Large Sunflowers

Diagram 1

Step 1

Embroider the centre of the Sunflower, using six strands of the recommended stranded thread. The centre must be a tight circle of colonial knots, Diagram 1.

Step 2

Embroider the Sunflower petals, using the recommended ribbon . A helpful hint, when embroidering the petals, is to draw a circle the size of the Sunflower with a water soluble pen,. Diagram 2. Embroider the petals next, following the numbers on Diagram 3. Each petal is one ribbon stitch. Make sure you do not pull this stitch too tight, as you will loose the loop on the end of the stitch. Embroider each ribbon stitch petal to the line you have drawn and all your petals will be the same length. Embroider one small straight stitch in the centre of each petal, at the base of each petal, using one strand of matching stranded thread.

Diagram 2

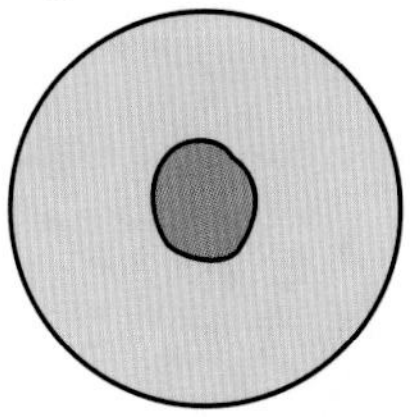

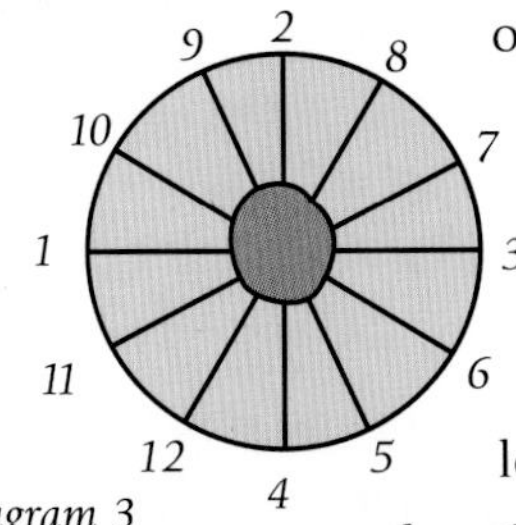

Diagram 3

The Large Sunflower Bud

Step 1

Embroider the top of the Sunflower bud, using closely embroidered colonial knots with six strands of the recommended stranded thread, Diagram 1.

Diagram 1

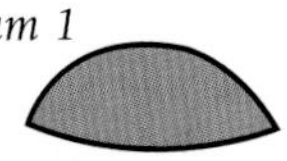

Diagram 2

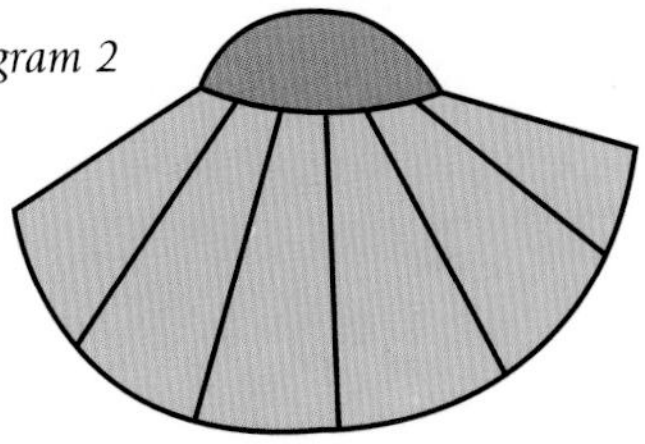

Step 2

Draw a half circle the size of your bud, with a water soluble pen, Diagram 2. Embroider the petals next, using ribbon stitch. Embroider one small straight stitch in the centre of each petal stitch, at the base of each petal, using one strand of matching stranded thread

The Large Daisies in Large Framing

Step 1

Embroider the centres of the daisies as per the separate instructions, using the recommended threads. All the centres of these Daisies are the same size and colour, Diagram 1.

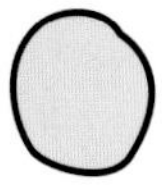

Diagram 1

Step 2

The Daisies are embroidered using 4mm, 7mm and 13mm wide silk ribbon. Check your design for the size ribbon used in each Daisy. The number in the centre of each Daisy indicates the ribbon size to be used for the petals. Each petal is one straight stitch which should not be pulled too tight. Remember this project is framed and the stretching used in the framing will pull your embroidery tight. Draw the circle for the petals using a water soluble pen. Each circle is the same size, but the number of petals will vary for each ribbon width. Make sure your silk ribbon lies flat on the fabric. There must be no twists in these stitches. The wider ribbon will fold where you take your straight stitch down, but this is fine. The main section of each petal must be flat. If you embroider the petals according to my diagrams they will be very evenly placed. I would suggest you stab stitch the straight stitches.

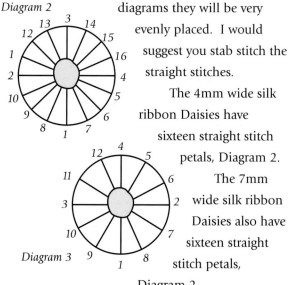

Diagram 2

Diagram 3

The 4mm wide silk ribbon Daisies have sixteen straight stitch petals, Diagram 2. The 7mm wide silk ribbon Daisies also have sixteen straight stitch petals, Diagram 2.

The13mm wide silk ribbon Daisies also have twelve straight stitch petals, Diagram 3.

Pistil Stitch

Bring the needle up through the fabric at A. Hold the needle horizontally

and wind the thread around the needle twice.

Turn the needle towards the fabric and insert it at B, about $^1/_4$" (5mm) from A. Hold the knot in place as you pull the needle and thread through the fabric.

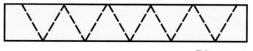

The Gardenia Flower
Step 1

Cut $19^1/_2$" (50cm) of 13mm wide silk ribbon. Using one strand of matching stranded thread and a No 9 Crewel needle, run a small running stitch along the ribbon in a wave like motion, Diagram 1. Secure your thread $^1/_2$"

Diagram 1

(1cm) in from the end of the silk ribbon. Stop stitching $^1/_2$" (1cm) from the end of the silk ribbon, but do not end this thread off. Remove the needle now, but do not cut the thread off.

Step 2

Using a stiletto, poke a hole in the fabric where you are going to embroider this flower. Secure the ribbon on the wrong side with one strand of matching stranded thread, do not cut this thread off. Bring this needle and thread to the right side of the fabric. You will now gather the silk ribbon in a little. Just gather the ribbon as you use it. Start stitching this ribbon onto the fabric with very small stab stitches. Stab stitching is just coming up and going back down through the fabric very close to where you came up with the stitch. Work in an anti-clockwise direction and you will be stitching from the inside to the outside, like a snail's shell, Diagram 2. The small stab stitches will be in the centre of the ribbon and they are very small so you will not see them. Try and push the ribbon up when you are stitching, so the flower has a raised effect. When you have used all the ribbon, poke another hole with the stiletto and take the ribbon to the wrong side, ending off securely. Thread the gathering thread back into the needle and take this thread to the wrong side, ending off securely. Do not worry if some flowers are larger than others. Remember all the flowers in a garden are not the same size.

Diagram 2

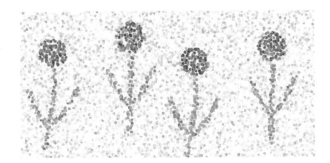

A Shoe Filled with Beautiful Flowers Cushion

This shoe is filled with a lovely pastel coloured flower arrangement. The soft tonings of the colours make this cushion a real show piece for a beautiful bedroom. This cushion is for the more experienced needle worker. The cushion's finished size is 11″ x 11″ (28cm x 28cm).

Requirements:
1 piece of cream silk dupion 20″ x 1yd 9″ (50cm x 115cm)
1 piece of cream cotton voile 13″ x 13″ (33cm x 33cm)
1 cream 8″ (20cm) zip
2yds 27″ (2.5 m) of cream cotton lace 1″ (2.5cm) wide
A small amount of Mill Hill glass seed beads No 00123 Cream
A small amount of Antique glass seed beads No 03019 Pink
1 packet of Mill Hill glass seed beads No 00161 Glitter Colours
A small amount of small cream pearl beads
1 small pink heart bead Mill Hill No 12086 Sm, Channel Heart
Needles: No 18 Chenille, No 9, 7 & 10 Crewel

1 spring hoop 7″ (18cm) in diameter.
Ribbons and Threads:
1 hank of Thread Gather 4mm wide silk ribbon No SR4034 A Child's Blush variegated Pale Pink and Cream
1 hank of Thread Gather 4mm wide silk ribbon No SR4033 Silver Queen, Pale Blue and Pink variegated
1 hank each of the following Thread Gather silk and wool thread No SPS063 Ivory & No SPS052-126 Dusky Pink
1 hank of Thread Gather pure silk thread No SNC033-037 variegated Pink and Blue
1 skein of DMC stranded thread No 523 Green, No 712 Cream, a small amount of No 800 Blue
1 skein of DMC Perle thread No 5-712 Cream.

Note:
   All silk ribbon embroidery has to be embroidered in a hoop using a No 18 Chenille needle. I embroider all my fine embroidery out of the hoop using either a No 9 or 7 Crewel needle. The glass seed beads should be sewn on using a No 10 Crewel needle. A No 18 Chenille needle should also be used for the Perle thread embroidery.

Step 1

Hand tack the cotton voile to the back of the silk fabric $^1/_2″$ (1cm) in from the raw edge. The silk tends to fray as you embroider, so it would be a good idea if you overlocked the edges now.

Step 2

Transfer the design as per the Transferring Instructions. Only transfer a small section at a time.

Step 3

You must embroider the whole outline of the shoe, even though parts of the shoe are covered with other embroidery. Embroider the shoe outline using whipped chain and Perle thread No 5-712. Make sure when you are whipping, you have enough thread to whip the entire section as you cannot join whipping. The heel of the shoe is filled with colonial knots using the Perle thread. Add a few glass seed beads No 00123 in with the colonial knots on the heel of the shoe.

Embroider the front of the shoe using the same thread. Embroider the Daisies first, using lazy daisy stitches and five even petals per daisy. Embroider one straight stitch in the centre of each petal with the same thread. Embroider the Daisy leaves, using the same thread. Each leaf is one fly stitch with a straight stitch in the centre of the fly stitch. Hand sew a small cream pearl bead in the centre of each daisy. Embroider the Forget-me-nots, using the same thread and each flower has four colonial knots very close together. Hand sew one glass seed bead No 00123 in the centre of each Forget-me-not using a No 10 Crewel needle and two strands of stranded thread No 712. Embroider the Lavender next, using the same thread. Each Lavender is two lazy daisy stitches at the top and one in the middle of the first two stitches and two colonial knots on the end. The stem of the Lavender is one straight stitch using the same thread.

Step 4

Embroider the loop stitch flowers, using 4mm wide silk ribbon No SR4034. Each flower will use 12″ (30cm) of silk ribbon. When you are embroidering this flower you will be using two needles. Use a No 18 Chenille needle for the silk ribbon and a No 9 Crewel needle for the straight stitches. Once you have embroidered one loop petal you must embroider one small straight stitch in the centre of the petal at the base of the petal, using one strand of stranded thread No 712. If you use this method you will not pull the loop stitch tight. Fill the centre of the loop stitch flower with glass seed beads No 00161. Make sure you pack the beads very heavy and close together, even on top of each other.

Embroider the leaves of the loop stitch flowers, using three strands of stranded thread No 523. Each leaf has two fly stitches on top of each other with one straight stitch in the centre of the last fly stitch.

Step 5

Embroider the stem stitch Roses next using two strands of the silk and wool

Shoe Outline

Loop Stitch Flowers

Ribbon Stitch Flowers

Lavender on Shoe

Bullion Stitch Rose

Stem Stitch Flowers

Forget-me-nots

Lazy Daisy Flowers

Forget-me-nots on Shoe

Leaf Vine

Daisy on Shoe

thread No SPS063 Ivory and No SPS052-126 Antique Rose. You will embroider two Antique Rose coloured stem stitch Roses and one Ivory stem stitch Rose. Please check separate instructions on how to embroider stem stitch Roses. Embroider the stem stitch Rose leaves next, using three strands of stranded thread No 523 and sets of two lazy daisy stitches.

Step 6

Embroider the ribbon stitch flowers, using 4mm wide silk ribbon No SR4033. Each flower has five even petals using ribbon stitch. Make sure you do not pull the loop of the ribbon stitch tight. Embroider a small straight stitch in the centre of each petal at the base of the petal using one thread of stranded thread No 800. Embroider the centre of the ribbon stitch flower, using one strand of the pure silk thread No SNC 033-037. This thread is made up of three strands and you only use one strand for these centres. The centre of the flower is one colonial knot. Embroider the leaf vine next, using three strands of stranded thread No 523 and feather stitch. You must embroider the feather stitch from the outside in.

Step 7

Embroider the silk thread lazy daisy flowers, using one strand of the silk thread No SNC003-037. Each flower has five even petals. The centre of the flower is one seed bead No 03019 pink.

Step 8

Embroider the Forget-me-nots, using the same thread as the above daisies. Each Forget-me-not has four colonial knots embroidered very close together. The centre of each Forget-me-not is one glass seed bead No 00123 cream. You might find you have more or less Forget-me-nots than me, because you embroidered them closer or further apart than me, but do not worry as my design is only a guide.

Step 9

Embroider the bullion Rose buds, using one strand of the silk thread No SNC003-037. This thread is made up of three strands and will separate very easily. Embroider the centre bullion stitch first, using a No 7 Crewel needle and one strand of the silk thread. This centre bullion has eleven twists. Embroider one bullion either side of the centre bullion, only this time use nine twists. This bullion is slightly shorter than the centre bullion. Test your tension for these bullion buds, as you might have to add twists or take twists away. My tension for bullion stitch is very tight. If you do

not like the needles I use, you can use the needle of your choice. Embroider all the buds in this manner. Embroider the greenery around the buds next, using one strand of stranded thread No 523. Bring your needle out above the centre bud to the left hand side, slide the needle under the centre bullion, but not through the fabric and take your needle into the fabric to the right of the centre bullion and through the fabric. Embroider one fly stitch around the bud, but do not extend the holding stitch. Embroider another fly stitch around the first fly stitch, this time extending the holding stitch back to the flowers to form the stems. Embroider a couple of small lazy daisy stitch leaves on the stems of the buds using the same thread. Please check your design as to which flowers the buds touch at the stem base. You will find the buds will all anchor into different flowers.

Step 10

It is a good idea to initial and date your embroidery. Hand sew the small pink bead heart near the flowers which have fallen onto the ground near the heel of the shoe. This cushion is made up the same as the Pedestal Cushion, only it does not have ribbon threaded through the lace and does not have a bow at the bottom. This cushion is the same size as the Pedestal Cushion.

The Australian wildflower framing

I am an Australian and I love Australian Wildflowers. Some people do not like the strong colours, but I love to promote these flowers in all my books. If you embroider on the Oatmeal Belfast Linen it will tone the bright colours down a lot. I hope you enjoy embroidering this beautiful piece of silk ribbon embroidery. I would not attempt this project as your very first project if you have never embroidered with silk ribbon before. This is a very beautiful project and is strictly for a framing. The finished size of the framing without the frame is 35cm long x 30cm wide or 14″x 12″. I would like to point out, the framing of the Map of Australia with silk ribbon wildflowers is not included as a project it has only been photographed. DMC owns this project and the design. It was designed and embroidered by me and I thought the two embroideries enhanced each other. If you would like more information on this embroidery, you should contact DMC Customer Service on 61 2 9559 5338.

Requirements:

1 piece of Belfast Linen Oatmeal No 3609-140-53 Zweigart 19″ x 17″ (48cm x 43cm)
1 piece of cream cotton voile 19$^1/_2$″ x 18″ (50cm x 45cm)
1 piece of cream cotton voile 9″ x 9″ (23cm x 23cm)
1 spring hoop 7″ (18cm) in diameter
Needles: Chenille No 18, Crewel No 9 & 7
2 lady bird buttons.

Ribbons and Threads:

1 card of Bucilla silk ribbon 7mm wide No 539 Red
1 card of Bucilla silk ribbon 4mm wide No 002 Black, No 629 Dark. Green, No 544 Light Pink, No 655 Creamy Yellow, No 653 Jungle Green, No 003 White, No 597 Brilliant Blue
1 card of Bucilla silk ribbon 7mm wide variegated No 2-7105 Daffodils
1 card of Bucilla silk ribbon 13mm wide variegated No 2-1315 Christmas Reds
2yds 27″ (2.5 m) of Kacoonda silk ribbon

7mm wide No 104 variegated Green
6yds 21″ (6 m) of Kacoonda silk ribbon
4mm wide No 108 variegated Dark Pinks
2yds 8″ (2 m) of Kacoonda silk ribbon
7mm wide No 107 variegated Light Greens
3yds 10$^1/_2$″ (3 m) of Kacoonda silk
ribbon 4mm wide No 8J variegated Pale
Greens
2yds 8″ (2 m) of Kacoonda silk ribbon
7mm wide No 4 variegated Creams Small
amounts of DMC stranded threads No
502 Blue Green, No 760 Medium Pink,
No 937 Medium Green, No 936 Dark
Green, No 524 Grey Green, No 796 Royal
Blue, No 445 Lemon, No Blanc, No 310
Black, No 937 Medium Dark Green, No
523 Light Grey Green, No 3045 Fawn, No
744 Yellow, No 3011 Dark Grassy Green,
No 712 Cream, No 743 Dark Yellow, No
745 Light Yellow
1 skein of DMC stranded thread No 111
variegated Golds, No 75 variegated Reds
A small amount of DMC No Art.273
Metallic thread Black & Gold
1 skein of DMC Perle thread No 5-676
Mustard Gold
2 lady bird buttons
A skein each of the following Rajmahal
threads No 45 Mustard, No 241 Dark
Pink, No 261 Pale Lemon.

Note:
Use a No 18 Chenille needle for the
silk ribbon and No 9 & 7 Crewel needles
for the fine embroidery. As this is a larger
project, I suggest you to follow my
instructions on transferring only one
section at a time and do not be in a great
hurry. It is a most enjoyable project if you
follow my instructions.

Step 1

Transfer the Waratah flower first.
Check how to transfer your design and
only transfer one section at a time. This is
one project where you must follow my
directions very carefully.

Mark the top section of the Waratah
first and embroider the centre with
colonial knots, using six strands
of stranded thread No 75. I use a
Chenille No 18
needle for
this section.
Should
you not like
this needle,
use the needle of your choice.
These colonial knots must be
packed in very tightly and the top
of the Waratah must be very full
with knots. It is lovely working with this
variegated thread as you never know
where the colours are going to come up.
It is not a good idea to embroider a
straight line of knots around the edge of
the top of the Waratah as you will get a
straight line in your embroidery. I usually
go all over the half circle with the knots,
as this gives a much better covering and it
does seem to fill up quicker if you follow
this method.

Cut 20″ (50cm) of 13mm wide silk
ribbon No 2-1315. Thread the No 9
Crewel needle with one strand of No 75
stranded thread. You will be running a
small running stitch in a wave like fashion
along the length of the 13mm wide silk
ribbon. Start your stitching $^1/_2$″ (1cm) in
from the raw end of the silk ribbon. Make
sure you embroider a couple of

Waratah

overstitches before you start, because if your running stitch comes out, you will have to embroider the running stitch again. Check the Stitch Guide for the Waratah flower instructions. The running stitch finishes $1/2"$ (1cm) in from the end of the silk ribbon. Thread another No 9 Crewel needle with one strand of the same thread. Poke a hole with a stiletto or knitting needle in the linen fabric at the left-hand corner, on the bottom of the colonial knots. Push the starting end of the silk ribbon (the end you anchored into first) into the hole and push the end of the ribbon through the hole to the wrong side. With the second needle, anchor the ribbon to the back of the fabric. End this thread off. Gather the remaining ribbon in so it fits snugly along the lower edge of the Waratah. Poke a hole in the right-hand corner of the lower edge, the same as the other side and anchor the end of the ribbon to the back of the fabric. End this thread off as well. Anchor this thread back where you started and using small stab stitches, catch the ribbon through the centre of the ribbon all the way along the bottom edge of the Waratah. Stab stitches are stitches which come up and then back through the fabric very close together.

Mark the outline of the Waratah now. Embroider the Waratah leaves, using 4mm wide silk ribbon No 629. The leaf is embroidered using a backstitch. Make sure you take the first and last section of the leaf under the Waratah flower. Embroider the vein of the leaf next, using continuous fly stitch down the centre of the leaf and two strands of stranded thread No 936.

Sturt's Desert Pea

Step 2

Transfer the Sturt's Desert Pea. Embroider the centre of the pea first, by working 10 colonial knots very close together. The knots are in two lines of five knots, using 4mm wide silk ribbon No 002. Embroider the petals next, using 7mm wide silk ribbon No 539. Stitch the bottom row of petals first. Begin with the centre petal, using a long lazy daisy stitch and extend the holding stitch a little longer. Embroider one straight stitch in the centre of the petal. Stitch one petal either side of the centre petal, in the same manner, but these petals are slightly smaller. Embroider the top row of petals the same way. Embroider the stem of the pea, using two strands of stranded thread No 936 and stem stitch. Embroider the leaves of the pea, using 4mm wide silk ribbon No 629. The leaves are one fly stitch with a straight stitch in the centre of the fly stitch.

Step 3

Transfer the Bottle Brush flower. To embroider the Bottle Brush, work the centre knots of the flowers first using Kacoonda 4mm wide silk ribbon No 8J.

Bottle Brush

Illustration only

The knots are colonial knots and about seven or eight knots are needed per flower. The knots are worked very closely together. Embroider five straight stitches at the end of each row of knots using the same silk ribbon. The centre straight stitch is longer and the two stitches either side are slightly smaller. Embroider the petals of the Bottle Brush flower next, using Kacoonda 4mm wide silk ribbon No 108. Each petal is one straight stitch very close together along the centre row of knots. Embroider the petals on either side of the knots in the same manner. Embroider one colonial knot on the end of each silk ribbon petal, using three strands of Rajmahal Art silk No 45. Each strand of the Art silk is made up of six strands so you will have to split the thread to three strands. Embroider the stems of the Bottle Brush next, using two strands of stranded thread No 523 and stem stitch. Embroider these stems all in the same direction. Embroider the leaves next, using 7mm wide Kacoonda silk ribbon No 104. Each leaf is a side ribbon stitch. Please check the Stitch Guide to see how you embroider this stitch. Embroider a small straight stitch in the centre of the ribbon stitch leaf, at the base of the leaf, using one strand of stranded thread No 523.

Step 4

Embroider the Flannel Flowers. Transfer the Flannel Flower positions now. Place the small piece of cotton voile into your frame and draw three circles using the water soluble pen. Please check the

Stitch Guide for the size of the circle. Embroider colonial knots using two strands of stranded thread No 524. This circle must be tightly packed with colonial knots. When you have completed your knots, cut the circle out with a small seam allowance. Turn the seam allowance into the centre and stitch down. Hand sew the circle of knots to the Flannel Flower positions on your design using two strands of stranded thread No 524. Embroider the petals next, using 7mm wide Kacoonda silk ribbon No 4. To help you keep your petals the same length, draw a circle the size of the Flannel Flower with your water soluble pen. If you only take your petals out to the circle edge, your petals will all end up the same length. The petals are straight stitches. Do not pull the stitches tight, just leave them sitting up slightly. Embroider the greenery around the petals next, using three strands of stranded thread No 524. The greenery around each petal is one fly stitch with the holding stitch extended a little longer.

Flannel Flower

Embroider the Flannel Flower leaves and stems next, using the same thread.

Embroider one straight stitch on the end of your leaf markings, then one fly stitch around the straight stitch. Using the same thread, embroider backstitches back to the flower to form the stem of the leaves. The stitches are approx $^1/_4''$ (4mm) in length. You must start the leaves and stems from the outside and work in. Embroider the other leaves coming out from the joins of the back

stitch. Check your design for the leaf markings. The leaves are one straight stitch and one fly stitch around the straight stitch, with the holding stitch extended back to the stem to form the stem of the leaf.

Step 5

Embroider the Everlasting Daisies. Transfer the positions for the Daisies now. Stitch the centres of the daisies, using the same method as the Flannel Flowers. Embroider the colonial knots using one strand of No 743 and one strand of No 745 blended in the one needle. This thread is variegated so you will get depths of colour through the knots. The circle of knots is the same size as well. Hand sew the finished circle of knots in the daisy positions. The petals of the Everlasting Daisy are worked with straight stitches, making sure the ribbon stays flat. Embroider the petals in the order marked in the Stitch Guide. The silk ribbon used in the Daisy petals is Bucilla 4mm wide silk ribbon No 003. Embroider one small straight stitch in the centre of each petal, at its base, using one strand of stranded thread No Blanc. Embroider the stems next, using two strands of stranded thread No 3011 and stem stitch. Make sure you embroider all the stems in the same direction. Embroider the Daisy leaves next, using 7mm wide Kacoonda silk ribbon No 107.

Everlasting Daisy

Each leaf is one slightly loose straight stitch. Embroider one very small straight stitch in the centre of each leaf, at its base, using one strand of stranded thread No 3011.

Step 6

Embroider the Tea Tree flowers. Transfer the Tea Tree flowers from your design. The flowers are five evenly placed lazy daisy stitches, using 4mm wide silk ribbon No 544. Each bud is one lazy daisy stitch, using the same silk ribbon. Tip each petal of the flowers and buds with a fly stitch and extend the holding stitch a little longer. The fly stitches are embroidered using three strands of stranded thread No 760. Embroider the centres of the flowers and one knot on the end of each bud, using two strands of stranded thread No 760 and two of stranded thread No 502. These four strands are all in the one needle. Embroider three colonial knots in the centre of each flower and one colonial knot on the end of each bud. Embroider the leaves next, using two strands of stranded thread No 502. The leaves are embroidered using continuous fly stitch, starting from the outside and working in.

Tea Tree Flower

Step 7

Embroider the Royal Blue Bell. Transfer the Blue Bell design now. The Blue Bell flowers are made up of five evenly placed lazy daisy stitches, using

4mm wide silk ribbon No 597. Each bud is one lazy daisy stitch, using the same ribbon. Tip each petal of the flowers and buds with a fly stitch and extend the holding stitch a little longer, using three strands of stranded thread No 796. Embroider the leaves next, using two strands of stranded thread No 937 and lazy daisy stitches, extending the holding stitch a little longer. Embroider the greenery around the buds next, using the same thread. Work one fly stitch around the bud, but do not extend the holding stitch. Embroider another fly stitch around the first fly stitch, this time extending the holding stitch back to the flowers to form the stem of the bud.

Royal Bluebell

Step 8

Embroider the Lemon Gum Blossom. Transfer the Gum Blossom now. Embroider the stems first, using two strands of stranded thread No 936 and stem stitch. Make sure you stitch the stems all in the same direction. Embroider a small half circle of buttonhole stitches at the end of each stem using the same thread. These stitches are stitched very close together. Embroider the petals next, using 4mm wide silk ribbon No 655. These stitches are straight stitches and also stitched very close together.

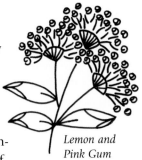

Lemon and Pink Gum

Embroider the first row of petals and then a second row of petals using the same ribbon, only this time the petals come from in-between the first row of petals and start halfway up the first row of petals. Embroider one colonial knot on the end of each petal, using three strands of Rajmahal Art silk No 261. This thread is made up of six strands and you must split the thread into three strands. Embroider the Lemon Gum Blossom leaves next, using Kacoonda 7mm wide silk ribbon No 104. Each leaf is one long side ribbon stitch. Please check your Stitch Guide for instructions on how to embroider the side ribbon stitch.

Step 9

Embroider the Pink Gum Blossom, using the instructions for the Lemon Gum Blossom. The stems and leaves are the same thread and ribbon. The petals will be pink, using the 4mm wide Kacoonda silk ribbon No 108. The colonial knots on the ends of each petal will be pink, using three strands of Rajmahal Art silk No 241.

Wattle

Step 10

Embroider the Wattle flowers. Transfer the Wattle flowers and stems now. Embroider the stems of the Wattle first, using two strands of stranded thread No 937 and stem stitch. Embroider the

Wattle flowers next using 7mm wide silk ribbon No 2-7105. Each Wattle flower is one very loose colonial knot. When you wind the ribbon around your needle, make sure the wraps are very loose and when you pull the ribbon through, do not tighten the ribbon as in a normal colonial knot. These knots might take a little practice. This ribbon is variegated, so you will get variation in colours as you embroider. Embroider the Wattle leaves next, using 4mm wide silk ribbon No 653. Each leaf is a small ribbon stitch. Embroider one very small straight stitch in the centre of each leaf, at the base of the leaf, using one thread of stranded thread No 937. Embroider the remaining Wattle Blossoms in the same manner.

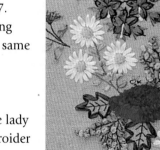

Step 11

Lady Beetle

Embroider the lady beetle's legs. Embroider six small straight stitches for each leg and one smaller straight stitch for the bend of the leg using two strands of stranded thread No 310. Please check the Stitch Guide for instructions on how to embroider the lady beetle's legs. Hand sew the lady beetle button onto the fabric over the embroidered legs.

Step 12

Embroider the Wheat. Transfer the Wheat now. Embroider the centre stem of the Wheat, using two strands of stranded thread No 3045 and stem stitch.

Wheat Ear

Embroider the wheat ears next, using three strands of stranded thread No 111. Each ear is one lazy daisy stitch with the holding stitch extended and one straight stitch in the centre of each lazy daisy stitch. Embroider the ears up the stem following your design. Embroider one straight stitch, in between the ears of wheat, with Perle thread No 5-676.

Step 13

Embroider the bees. The body of each bee is seven satin stitches worked very closely together, using three strands of stranded thread No 744. Embroider the bee's stripes next using two strands of stranded thread No 310. Embroider one very small fly stitch around the end of the bee's body and extend the holding stitch a little to form the bee's sting. Embroider one straight stitch over the bee's body where you started your fly stitch. Embroider another straight stitch over the bee's body at the front of the body and then yet another straight stitch over the body in between the two stripes you have already embroidered. Please check your Stitch Guide on how to embroider the bees. Embroider the bee's legs next, using the same thread. The legs are two small

Small Bee

straight stitches in the shape of a V. Embroider the bee's eyes next, using the same thread and embroider two colonial knots very close together at the front end of the body. Embroider the feelers next, using the same thread. The feelers are two straight stitches in the shape of a V in between the bee's eyes. It is easier to embroider the feelers if you start the stitch from the outside and go between the eyes. Embroider the bee's wings next, using

DMC Metallic thread No Art 273. Each bee has two wings on the top of its body and each wing is one lazy daisy stitch with the holding stitch slightly extended. Repeat for the second bee.

Step 14

It is a good idea to initial and date your embroidery. Have your embroidery framed in your own style of framing.

The Ruby Rose
Pincushion

I f you are an embroiderer this pincushion will be a beautiful addition to your sewing utensils. It could also be used as a brooch holder. What a beautiful gift to give an embroiderer.

Requirements:
8" x 8" (20cm x 20cm) of cream wool flannel
8" x 8" (20cm x 20cm) of maroon velvet
24" (60cm) of maroon braid
1 lady bird button
1 gold charm needle, thimble, scissors and cotton reel
Toy filling or wool scraps
Craft glue
1 plastic spray can lid, a small tin could also be used (You will need some small rocks to fill the spray can lid to weight it down)
Needles: Chenille No 18 & Crewel No 9
1 spring hoop 5" (13cm) in diameter
12" (30cm) of (10mm) **or** $^3/_8$" wide maroon double sided satin ribbon.

Ribbons and Threads:
1 card of Bucilla silk ribbon 13mm wide No 2-1306 Burgundies variegated
1 card of Bucilla silk ribbon 7mm wide No 2-7102 Jungle Greens variegated
1 card of Bucilla silk ribbon 4mm wide No 501 Off White, No 656 Lemon Yellow, No 042 Maroon
$^1/_2$ skein of DMC stranded thread No 936 Dark Green, No 712 Cream, No 815 Maroon, No 310 Black
A small amount of DMC Gold thread No Art.282
4 threads of DMC Perle thread No 5-712 Cream to hand sew the pincushion.

Note:
This silk ribbon embroidery is slightly different because you do not use the cotton voile at the back of the wool flannel. You must still embroider the silk ribbon in a hoop.

Step 1
Transfer the design as per Transferring Instructions. Only transfer a small section at a time. Do not cut the wool flannel pincushion circle out until you have finished your embroidery.

Step 2

Embroider the ruby red Roses first. Work the Roses, using 13mm wide silk ribbon No 2-1306. Each Rose uses 12" (30cm) of silk ribbon. Check your Stitch Guide on how to embroider the Roses/Carnations. The Roses are embroidered using DMC stranded thread No 815. The Rose leaves are embroidered using 7mm wide silk ribbon No 2-7102. The leaves are embroidered in sets of two and each leaf is one loop stitch. Check the Stitch Guide for instructions on how to embroider loop stitch. Embroider one small straight stitch in the centre of the loop stitch, at the base of the leaf, using one strand of stranded thread No 936.

Red Rose or Carnation

Step 3

Embroider the cream lazy daisy flowers, using 4mm wide silk ribbon No 501. Each flower has five evenly spaced lazy daisy petals. Each bud is one lazy daisy stitch. The centre of the Daisy is one colonial knot, using 4mm wide silk ribbon No 656. Embroider the Daisy leaves next, using two strands of stranded thread No 936. Each leaf is one lazy daisy stitch with the holding stitch extended a little longer. Embroider the greenery around the buds next, using the same thread. Embroider one fly stitch around each bud and extend the holding stitch back to the Daisy flower.

Cream Daisy

Step 4

Embroider the vine, using two strands of stranded thread No 936 and feather stitch. To embroider the feather stitch, you must start from the outside and embroider in. Embroider the flowers on the vine next, using 4mm wide silk ribbon No 042. Each flower is one colonial knot.

Embroidered Vine

Step 5

Embroider the lady bird's legs following the instructions in the Stitch Guide. The legs are embroidered using two strands of stranded thread No 310. Hand sew the lady bird button in the centre of the embroidered legs.

Lady Beetle

Step 6

Embroider the chain for the charms, using DMC gold thread No Art 282 and continuous chain stitch. It is a good idea when embroidering with gold thread to use a large eyed needle, so the thread does not deteriorate. I use a No 18 Chenille needle for this thread. Hand sew the charms to the chain using the gold thread.

If the holes in the charms are a little small for the eye of your needle, you can still sew them on with the gold thread. Simply bring your needle up through the fabric, unthread it, pass the thread through the hole in the charm and then rethread your needle and continue onto the next charm. Repeat this method for all the charms.

Step 7

It is a good idea to initial and date your embroidery.

Assembling the Pincushion

Step 1

Cut the wool flannel circle for the pincushion top out now. Cut the velvet base circle out now as well. With the Perle thread No 5-712, work a small running stitch around the embroidered circle about $1/2$" (1cm) in from the raw edge. You can start with a knot in your thread, but you should also do two or three overstitches to hold the thread firm. This thread is going to be used to gather this edge in and has to be able to withstand a great deal of strain. Do not end off this thread or cut off the needle.

Step 2

Draw up the gathering thread until you have a circle which will fit on top of your spray can lid, secure with a couple of overstitches and then finish off. Do not gather the circle too tight, or it will not fit properly on top of your pincushion base.

Step 3

Start stuffing the toy filling or wool scraps into the top of the pincushion. You will end up with a giant mushroom shape. Use the end of a wooden spoon to push the filling firmly into the mushroom. The firmer the better.

Step 4

Take the Chenille needle and the Perle thread and work a small running stitch around the velvet circle, about $1/2$" (1cm) in from the raw edge. Start with a knot in the thread, but also do two or three overstitches to hold the thread firm. It is going to be used to gather the edge and will have to withstand a great deal of strain.

Step 5

Fill the spray can lid with small rocks, enough to weight it down. Place the spray can lid inside the velvet circle and gather in the velvet tightly. The velvet will come over the top of the spray can lid. Secure the thread off with a couple of overstitches.

Step 6

With the Chenille needle and the Perle thread, ladder stitch the embroidered top of the pincushion to the velvet base of the pincushion. Secure the thread off once you have completely sewn the top to the bottom.

Step 7

Take the maroon braid and glue the braid to the bottom edge of the velvet base and then glue another row of braid to the velvet where the embroidered sections meets the velvet base. Tie a small bow, with 10mm wide satin ribbon and glue this bow over the join of the top row of braid. You have now completed your pincushion.

Illustration only

The Ruby Rose
Scissor Case

Well! If you have just embroidered the pincushion, what a lovely partner this scissor case would make. If you gave this away as a present to an embroiderer, I think you would have a good friend forever. The two pieces side by side make a beautiful gift. If you have a very expensive pair of scissors, this case will help protect them from damage if they are dropped on the floor.

Requirements:
19^1/$_2$" x 8" (50cm x 20cm)of cream wool flannel
Template plastic, half a sheet will be enough
1 scissor charm
Needles: Chenille No 18 & Crewel No 9
1 lady bird button
Make or purchase a small tassel for the bottom of the scissor case
Make or purchase a gold cord (DMC Gold stranded thread No 5282
makes great cords and tassels)
Crochet hooks: No .60 & No 1.

Ribbons and Threads:
The threads and ribbons are the same as the pincushion. If you completed the pincushion you might have some left over, if not, purchase the same threads given for the pincushion.
1 ball of crochet cotton No 8-Ecru Cream.

Step 1
It is a good idea not to cut the shape of the scissor case out first, as the embroidery has to be stitched in a hoop. You will find it much easier to embroider if you do not cut the shape out first. Please draw all sections to make sure you have enough fabric.

Step 2
Follow the embroidery instructions for the pincushion, except embroider the design for the scissor case. The scissor case does not have all the charms the pincushion has.

Step 3
Once you have finished your embroidery, mark the outline of the front scissor case with a water soluble pen. You can cut this fabric out, but leave extra fabric around the outline of the scissor case. Take another piece of wool flannel the same size as the embroidered section with the same extra fabric around the

outline and place it at the back of the embroidered section. Take the template plastic and cut the front scissor case pattern out just slightly smaller than the pattern. Sandwich the template plastic in between the embroidered section and the plain section of the front of the scissor case. Pin around the outline of the front scissor case. Hand sew a small running stitch around the outline of the front scissor case. This running stitch will stay in, so use a single strand of stranded thread No 712 cream.

Once you have completed your running stitch, machine a row of stitching over the top of the running stitch. The template plastic is now sealed inside the wool flannel. Cut the extra fabric away now but leave about $^3/_{16}$″ (3-4mm) from the machine stitch line. Now is the time to crochet around the edge of the front scissor case.

Using the .60 crochet hook and the ball of DMC crochet cotton, crochet a row of double crochet around the front scissor case. Start the crocheting where I have marked on your pattern. The reason I use this small hook first, is to make it easier to push the hook through the fabric. You might have to adjust your tension, my crochet is very tight.

Change to the No 1 hook for the second row. This row is another double crochet row.

The next row is the fancy edge.

*1 treble into the next double crochet, 1 chain, a picot of 4 chain, 1 chain, 1 treble into the same double crochet, 3 chain, miss 2 double crochet, repeat from *

Step 4

Repeat the same instructions for the back, but the fancy edge only goes across the top of the back scissor case.

Crochet the two rows of double crochet, starting where marked on your pattern. Crochet the fancy edge from where it is marked on your pattern.

Red Rose or Carnation

Step 5

End off the crochet securely. It is now time to iron the crocheted edge. I use spray starch to make my crochet firm. If you do not starch the crocheted edge it will be very limp. I usually spray the starch onto a small plate and using my fingers, I dab the crocheted edge with the starch. If you follow this method you will avoid the starch going onto the wool flannel. Once you have dabbed the starch all around the crochet, iron the crochet from the wrong side first, then iron from the right side. Keep ironing until all

the starch is completely dry. Once you have followed this step once, you will not have to do this again until you have to wash the scissor case and if you are like me, I use my scissor case and in time it does get dirty. By using the template plastic, the scissor case is completely washable. Hand wash and drip dry of course. Repeat this step with the starch for the back of the scissor case.

Cream Daisy

Step 6

It is now time to hand sew the scissor case together. If you are having a tassel on the end of the case, now is the time to make or purchase it, then stitch it on the inside of the front so it will hang from the bottom of the scissor case. I have made a tassel out of the crochet

cotton and decorated the top of the tassel with small glass cream seed beads. Pin the front of the scissor case to the back of the scissor case making sure the back scissor case has the right side of the crochet facing the front. Thread the needle with some of the crochet cotton and stab stitch the front scissor case to the back scissor case. Stab stitching is just coming up and going back down very close to where you came up. The stitches are quite close together. Make sure you secure the front scissor case at the corners very well, as there will be a lot of stress and strain on these points. Make a cord, or purchase some ribbon, to tie the scissors on. Make a gold cord or purchase some cord to hang the scissor case around your neck.

Embroidered Vine

Lady Beetle

*A Beautiful
Lavender Bag*

This Lavender bag is one of my favourites. It is very simple and the flower arrangement is just so sweet. This bag could have many uses besides a Lavender bag. You do not need too much experience to embroider this project. Please note, as this is only a very quick project, I did not put any voile at the back of the silk ribbon embroidery. I do not break this rule very often, but I have in this project. If I had used different silk ribbon stitches I would have definitely put voile on the back. The Lavender bag size is $7^1/_2$" x 6" (19cm x 15cm) approx. The fabric measurements are larger than you require.

Requirements:
1 piece of 14" x 12" (35cm x 30cm) Olympia linen, Ecru
1 piece 8" x 14" (20cm x 35cm) of cream cotton voile for the lining
1 spring hoop 5" (13cm) in diameter
Needles: Chenille No 18 & Crewel No 9 & 7.

Ribbons and Threads:
1 card of Bucilla silk ribbon 7mm wide
No 024 Lavender, No 574 Periwinkle
1 card of Bucilla silk ribbon 4mm wide
No 633 Pale Hunter
Small amounts of DMC stranded thread
No 712 Cream, No 3053 Pale Green, No 211 Pale Mauve
1 skein of DMC Perle thread No 5-712 Cream for the cords.

Note:
You must embroider all the silk ribbon in a hoop. The fine embroidery can be embroidered out of the hoop. You might wish to purchase the cord for the bag, or make it, but 3mm wide double sided satin ribbon would look very good as well. I use No 7 Crewel needles for the bullion stitches but if you do not like these needles, use the needle of your choice.

Step 1
Transfer your design as per Transferring Instructions. Only transfer small sections at a time.

Step 2

Embroider the stems of the Lavender flowers, using two strands of stranded thread No 3053 and stem stitch.

Step 3

Embroider the Lavender flowers, using 7mm wide silk ribbon No 024 and embroider five petals evenly spaced using loop stitch. Please check your Stitch Guide for instructions on how to embroider loop stitch.

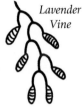

Loop Stitch Flowers

Stem

Leaf

Loop Stitch Bud

Embroider one very small straight stitch in the centre of the loop stitch, at its base, using one strand of stranded thread No 211. Each bud is one loop stitch, make sure you catch this loop with the same straight stitch as the flower.

Embroider one colonial knot in the centre of each flower, using the 7mm wide silk ribbon No 574. Embroider the greenery around the buds next, using two strands of stranded thread No 3053. Embroider one fly stitch around each bud, do not extend the holding stitch.

Step 4

Embroider the leaves, using 4mm wide silk ribbon No 633. Each leaf is one lazy daisy stitch.

Step 5

Embroider the Lavender stems, using two strands of stranded thread No 3053.

Each stem is feather stitch. When you embroider feather stitch, you must start from the outside and embroider in. Embroider the Lavender flowers next, using two strands of stranded thread No 211 and one thread of No 3053. All these strands are in the one No 7 Crewel needle. Each flower is one bullion stitch with nine twists. Embroider the flowers where marked on your design.

Lavender Vine

Step 6

It is a good idea to initial and date your embroidery.

Step 7

Embroider the buttonhole eyelets where they are marked on your design. You will have four eyelet holes. Each eyelet is embroidered using two strands of stranded thread No 712 and button hole stitch all around the hole. To make the hole use a stiletto or a knitting needle. These tools will make the hole but not break the fabric.

How to Make Up the Lavender Bag:
Step 1

Cut the linen to the pattern size. You will have two pieces of linen and two pieces of cotton voile.

Step 2

Machine the cotton voile to the end without the embroidery (this is the top of the bag) with the right sides of the fabric facing each other. Place the back of the

bag and the front of the bag, right sides together and pin along the long sides of the voile, then the linen, then across the bottom of the bag with the linen, then up the long linen side, then up the voile long side. Do not pin across the top of the voile.

Step 3

Machine a line of stitching $^1/_4''$ (5mm) in from the raw edge, all the way round the bag but not across the bottom of the voile.

Step 4

Turn the bag through the open voile bag. Turn the bag over at the top edge, where marked on your pattern, and pin around that top edge. You are now going to make the casing for the cord or ribbon to go through. Machine the first row of stitching where marked on your pattern. Machine a second row of stitching where marked on your pattern. If you place the machine stitches where the measurements are, your eyelets should be in the centre of the casing. If your eyelets are not in the centre of the casing you have made a measurement mistake.

Step 5

Turn the raw edge of the voile in, about $^1/_2''$ (1cm) and machine across the bottom of the voile bag.

Step 6

Make the cord using the Perle thread No 5-712 or thread 3mm wide double sided satin ribbon through the eyelet holes. Thread one cord around one way and the other cord around the other way.

By threading in this way, your bag will not come open unless you pull it open. Tie knots in the two ends.

The Pink Chrysanthemum Lavender Bag

This Lavender bag is a little more elegant than the previous one. This version has more embroidery than the other bag and has a crocheted edge. You will need a little more experience for this project. The size is $8^1/_2''$ x $5^3/_4''$ (21cm x 14.5cm).

Requirements:
12″ x 14″ (30cm x 35cm) of Olympia linen, Ecru
$19^1/_2''$ x 1yd 9″ (50cm x 115cm) approx of cream cotton voile
1 spring hoop 5″ (13cm) in diameter
Needles: Chenille No 18 & No 9 Crewel.

Ribbons and Threads:
1 card of Bucilla silk ribbon 7mm wide
No 2-7113 Baby Pinks
1 card of Bucilla silk ribbon 4mm wide
No 531 Light Coral, No 003 White, No
633 Pale Hunter, No 656 Lemon Yellow
Small amounts of DMC stranded thread
No 712 Cream, No Blanc, No 225 Pale
Pink, No 522 Medium Green, No 224
Medium Pink
1 skein of DMC Perle thread No 712
Cream for the cords
1 ball of DMC crochet cotton No 8-Ecru.

Note:
This Lavender bag has to have the voile at the back of the embroidered section. All silk ribbon embroidery is to be embroidered in a hoop. Fine embroidery can be embroidered out of the hoop.

Step 1
Cut the two pieces of Olympia linen for the Lavender bag as per pattern. Hand tack the cotton voile to the back of the linen which is going to be embroidered, about $^1/_2$" (1cm) in from the raw edge.

Step 2
You will make the centre of the Chrysanthemum first, using a small piece of cream cotton voile 8″ x 8″ (20cm x 20cm) approx. Draw the circle the same size as the pattern. Fill the circle with colonial knots using six strands of stranded thread No 224. It is best to embroider the knots in a hoop using a No 18 Chenille needle. If you are not happy with this needle, use the needle of your choice. Fill this circle very full with knots. Once you have completed your colonial knots, cut the excess fabric away leaving a small seam allowance. Please check the Stitch Guide on how to embroider the Chrysanthemum. Fold the seam allowance into the centre of the circle with two strands of the same stranded thread as the knots.

Chrysanthemum Flower

Step 3
Transfer the position for the Chrysanthemum first and embroider the centre to the linen fabric using the same thread as the knots. The centre is stab stitched to the linen fabric and it is best embroidered in the hoop.

Step 4
Draw a circle, with the water soluble pen, around the Chrysanthemum centre. This line will keep your petals all the same size. The next section of the flower is embroidered the same as the Waratah in the Australian Wildflower Framing. The frill of this flower is made from 17 $^3/_4$″ (45cm) of 7mm wide silk ribbon. Embroider a wave like running stitch along the full length of the silk ribbon, starting with a knot and overstitch approx. $^1/_2$" (1cm) in from the end of the ribbon.

Stop the running stitch $^1/_2$″ (1cm) from the other end, but do not end this thread off. You will use one strand of stranded thread No 225 for the running stitch. Gather the ribbon in to fit around the centre of the Chrysanthemum. With a stiletto or knitting needle, make a hole in the linen close to the edge of the centre of the flower and push the two raw edges of the ribbon through the hole. Secure the ribbon on the back side of the fabric with a couple of overstitches using one strand of stranded thread No 225. Using the same thread, stitch the gathered frill around the centre knots using a small straight stitch in the centre of the frill. Embroider the ribbon stitch outside petals, using 7mm wide silk ribbon No 2-7113. Take the ribbon stitch petals out to the line you drew with the water soluble pen earlier. Embroider the petals as per diagram in the Stitch Guide on how to embroider the Chrysanthemum. Embroider one small straight stitch in each petal, at its base, using one strand of stranded thread No 225.

Step 5

Embroider the Chrysanthemum leaves, using 4mm wide silk ribbon No 633. Each set of leaves is three lazy daisy stitches. Check the design for the positions.

Step 6

Embroider the coral coloured Daisies, using 4mm wide silk ribbon No 531. Each Daisy is made up of five

Daisy and Buds

evenly placed lazy daisy stitch petals. Embroider one lazy daisy stitch for each bud. Embroider the Daisy leaves next, using two strands of stranded thread No 522. Each leaf is one lazy daisy stitch with the holding stitch extended a little longer. Embroider the greenery around the buds next using the same thread. Embroider one fly stitch around the bud and extend the holding stitch back to the Daisy to form the stem.

Leaves

Step 7

Embroider the feather stitch vine, using two strands of stranded thread No 522 and feather stitch. Make sure you start the feather stitch from the outside and work in. Embroider the flowers where marked on your design next, using 4mm wide silk ribbon No 531 and one colonial knot for each flower.

Feather Stitch Vine

Step 8

Embroider the Orchids. Embroider the Orchid centre, using 4mm wide silk ribbon No 531 and one colonial knot for each Orchid centre. Embroider the petal around the centre of the Orchid next, using 4mm wide silk ribbon No 003. The silk ribbon has to be threaded double in the needle. I still use the No 18 Chenille needle even though the ribbon is threaded double. Embroider one loose straight stitch either side of the centre knot, then work the other Orchid petals in the same manner. Embroider the stems of the

Orchids

71

Orchids next, using two strands of stranded thread No 522. Starting at the top centre petal, embroider one small buttonhole stitch through the two ribbon straight stitches, sliding the needle under the ribbon of the two straight stitches. Using the same thread, backstitch the stem back to the Chrysanthemum. Embroider the remaining flowers in the same way, but check the design for the position of the flower stems.

Step 9

It is a good idea to initial and date your embroidery.

How to Make Up Your Lavender Bag

Note:

The making up of this bag is slightly different because it has a crocheted edge.

Step 1

Run a line of machine stitches along the fold line on the top, of the embroidered front section only.

Step 2

Machine the cotton voile lining to the top edge of the front of the Lavender bag and the top edge of back of the Lavender bag, using a $^1/_4$″ (5mm) seam allowance.

Step 3

Embroider the eyelet holes in the top of the Lavender bag now, following Step 7 from the previous Lavender bag. Use the same thread and check your pattern design for the eyelet positions.

Step 4

Place the front embroidered section and the back plain section, right sides together and pin around the outside edge. Pin down the voile, down the linen, across the bottom of the linen, up the linen, up the voile but do not pin across the voile. Leave the end open. Machine around where you have just pinned with a $^1/_4$″ (5mm) seam allowance.

Step 5

Turn the bag to the right side, through the opening in the voile. Pin along the fold line. Check the pattern for position. Machine a stitch line along the marking on your pattern for the first row of stitching for the cord casing. Machine stitch the second row for the casing, where marked on your pattern.

Step 6

Turn the raw edges of the voile in and machine stitch across the bottom of the voile lining bag. The seam allowance is $^1/_2$″(1cm).

How to Crochet the Edge

Note:

Now is the time to crochet the edge. Use the ball of DMC crochet cotton No 8-Ecru for the crocheting. I use the No .60 crochet hook for the first row of crochet only, as it is a fine hook and will go through the fabric a little easier. The No 1 hook is used for all the other rows.

Step 1

1st. row: (Using the No .60 hook).
1 double crochet all around the
top of the Lavender bag.

2nd. row: (Change to the No 1 hook).
Crochet another double crochet
row around the previous row of
double crochet.

3rd. row: *1 treble into the next double
crochet, 4 chain, 1 treble into
the same double crochet, 4
chain, miss 3 double crochet,
repeat from *

4th. row: *1 treble into the 4 chain which
is in-between the two trebles of
the previous row, 4 chain, 1
treble into the same 4 chain, 4
chain, 1 double crochet into the
four chain loop, 4 chain repeat
from*

5th. row: crochet 4 chain, 1 double
crochet over every loop of the
previous row.

End all the ends of the crochet
off securely.

Thread the cords you have made, or
ribbon you have purchased, through the
eyelet holes. Thread one cord one way
and thread the other cord the other way.
Tie a knot in the cord ends. The reason
you thread this way is so the bag cords
will not open unless you pull them open.

Illustration only

Large Framing
with White Daisies
in a Cameo Vase

This framing is one of my favourite projects. It is a very large framing and the photo does not show it in full. I felt it was more important you have a close up of the embroidery. It was the last project I embroidered for this book and I enjoyed every stitch I put in it. What a lovely way to finish off my book. The Daisies look as though they are alive. The porcelain cameo is a beautiful addition to the vase. I love the colours of this framing and they will tone in with most colours in your home. Make sure you have this project professionally framed by an experienced embroidery framer. I hope you enjoy this project as much I did. The finished size, without the frame, is 17″ x 22″ (43cm x 56cm). I have already included in the requirement list, the extra fabric needed for framing.

Requirements:
1 piece of Quakers Cloth No 3993-140-718 Zweigart 24″ x 28″ (60cm x 71cm)
1 piece of cream cotton voile 25″x 30″ (65cm x 76cm)
1 small piece of cream cotton voile to make the Daisy centres 8″ x 8″ (20cm x 20cm)
1 spring hoop 7″ (18cm) in diameter
Needles: Chenille No 18, No 14 darner, No 7, 9 & 10 Crewel
1 cameo to match the embroidery
$^1/_2$ string of small cream pearl beads
1 packet of Mill Hill glass seed beads No 00123 Cream
3 small opaque butterflies.

Ribbons & Threads:
3 cards of Bucilla 13mm wide silk ribbon No 1320 White
2 cards of Bucilla 7mm wide silk ribbon No 003 White
2 cards of Bucilla 4mm wide silk ribbon No 003 White
2 cards of Bucilla 4mm wide silk ribbon No 271 Aqua
4yds 14″ (4 m) of Kacoonda 4mm wide silk ribbon variegated Greens No 8J
1 skein of DMC Perle thread No 5-928 Pale Blue Grey
1 skein of DMC Perle thread No 3-928 Pale Blue Grey
1 skein of DMC stranded thread No 523 Green, No (Blanc) White, No 744 Yellow, No 712 Cream.

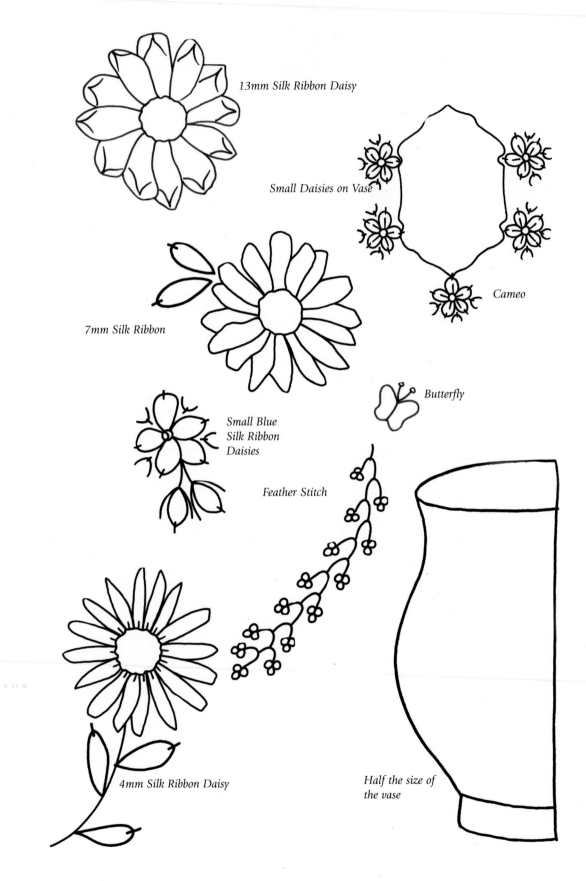

13mm Silk Ribbon Daisy

Small Daisies on Vase

Cameo

7mm Silk Ribbon

Butterfly

Small Blue
Silk Ribbon
Daisies

Feather Stitch

4mm Silk Ribbon Daisy

Half the size of
the vase

Note:

All the silk ribbon is embroidered in a frame. Use the No 18 Chenille needle for the 4mm and 7mm wide silk ribbon but use the No 14 darner for the 13mm wide silk ribbon. The centres of the Daisies are embroidered on a separate piece of cotton voile in a hoop. All fine embroidery is embroidered out of the hoop. Do not sew the cameo on until you have finished all your embroidery.

Step 1

Hand tack the cotton voile to the back of the linen fabric, $^{1}/_{2}$″ (1cm) in from the raw edge.

Step 2

Transfer the vase onto the linen fabric first. Check Transferring Instructions on how to transfer the design. While you do not see all the vase, you must embroider the whole outline. Work continuous chain stitch around the outside of the vase and across the bottom section of the vase, using Perle No 5-928. Whip the chain, using Perle No 3-928. Fill the bottom section of the vase with colonial knots using Perle thread No 5-928. Embroider the knots on the vase, using Perle thread No 5-928 and colonial knots. Embroider the Daisies on the vase, using the same thread. Each Daisy has five evenly placed lazy daisy stitches. Embroider one straight stitch in the centre of each petal, using the same thread. Each Daisy centre is one cream pearl bead. The

Daisy leaves are one fly stitch, using the same thread.

Step 3

Take the small piece of cotton voile and place it in your hoop. Embroider the centres of the Daisies, using three strands of stranded thread No 744 and the No 7 Crewel needle. Embroider the colonial knots in a hoop and check the Stitch Guide for the size of the centre circles. Fill the circles very full of knots. Once you have finished filling the centres, cut the centre out of the voile making sure you leave a small seam allowance around the circle of knots. Using the same thread, turn the seam allowance into the centre of the circle and catch the seam allowance down. Stab stitch the centre onto the linen fabric where marked on your design. Embroider all the centres first before you cut any out (you will loose the tension if you cut any out before you have embroidered them all).

Step 4

Check your design very carefully, because some of the Daisies are embroidered using 4mm, some 7mm and others 13mm wide silk ribbon. Only use 12″ (30cm) of silk ribbon at a time. The position of the thickness of the ribbon in this design is very important. A handy hint to keep the petals all the one length is to draw, with a water soluble pen, a circle the size of the Daisy you are

embroidering. Take the petals out to the line of the circle and you will have all your petals even. Embroider the petals in the numbered order. Check your Stitch Guide to see how you embroider the white Daisies. All the Daisies are embroidered using straight stitches. The 4mm wide silk ribbon Daisies are pulled quite firm but not tight. The 7mm wide silk ribbon Daisies are a little looser. The 13mm wide silk ribbon Daisies are quite loose. If you have never embroidered with the wide silk ribbon before, it might be a good idea to have a practice first. They are not difficult, but a little patience and practice will reward you in the end. Once you have embroidered the petals, work one small straight stitch in the centre of each petal, at the base of the petal, using one strand of stranded thread No Blanc (white). Embroider the Daisy stems, using two strands of stranded thread No 523 and stem stitch. Make sure you embroider all the stems from the bottom up.

Step 5

Embroider the Daisy leaves next using 4mm wide silk ribbon No 8J. Each leaf is one lazy daisy stitch with the holding stitch extended a little longer.

Step 6

Embroider the blue Daisy flowers, using 4mm wide silk ribbon No 271. Each Daisy has five even petals in lazy daisy stitch and each bud is one lazy daisy

stitch. The centres of the Daisies are one colonial knot using six strands of stranded thread No 744. Embroider the leaves of the blue Daisies next, using two strands of stranded thread No 523. The leaves are one fly stitch. Embroider the greenery around the buds, using the same thread and embroider one fly stitch around the bud, extending the holding stitch back to the Daisy to form the stem of the bud.

Step 7

Embroider the feather stitch vines, using two strands of stranded thread No 523 and feather stitch. It is important you embroider this stitch from the outside in. Using two strands of stranded thread No 712, hand sew three glass seed beads No 00123 Mill Hill, on the end of each spoke of the feather stitch. Each bead must be sewn on separately.

Step 8

Hand sew the butterflies in position, using two strands of stranded thread No 712 cream. Embroider the feelers next, using the same thread. Each feeler is one straight stitch with a colonial knot on the end of the straight stitch. It is a good idea to initial and date your embroidery. Hand sew the cameo on now, using two strands of stranded thread No 712 and the No 9 Crewel needle. Bring the needle up

through the hole in the cameo and then place a small cream pearl bead on the needle. Take the needle back through the hole in the cameo and through to the wrong side of the linen. Try and take the needle back up through the bead again to secure the cameo a little more. Repeat this step for the hole at the bottom of the cameo. I do not recommend you glue the cameo on, as the glue could affect your fabric.

Step 9

Have your embroidery framed professionally.

The Elegance of the Cream Evening Bag

This elegant evening bag is just what you need when you are all dressed up for something special, the perfect finishing touch. It would also make a beautiful accessory for that special wedding day. Instead of flowers, why not this beautiful wedding bag. The crocheted edge gives the bag an elegant finishing touch. This bag could also be embroidered using pure white silk fabric and white silk ribbon. I would like to tell you a little about the ribbon colour I used in this project. I designed this colour quite a few years ago, with Kacoonda, as I embroider with cream on cream a lot. Kacoonda liked the colour so much they decided to incorporate it into their entire range of threads and ribbons. I find this colour goes with everything, it just seems to blend in perfectly. Evening bag size 10 $^1/_2$″ x 19 $^1/_2$″ (27cm x 50cm).

Requirements:
2 pieces of cream silk dupion fabric 21$^1/_2$″ x 12″ (55cm x 30cm) for the bag
2 pieces of cream silk dupion fabric 6″ x 6″ (15cm x 15cm)for the base of the bag

1 piece of cream cotton voile 24″ x 14″ (60cm x 35cm)
1 piece of template plastic 6″ x 6″ (15cm x 15cm) inside the bottom base
4 large cream pearl beads for the base of the bag
1 string of cream medium size pearl beads
1 packet of cream DMC glass seed beads No 712 Cream
1 spring hoop 7″ (18cm) in diameter
Crochet hooks, No .60 & No 1
1 square of wadding 6″ x 6″ (15cm x 15cm)
Needles: No 18 Chenille, No 9 & 10 Crewel.

Ribbons & Threads:
2yds 8″ (2 m) of Kacoonda 13mm wide silk ribbon No 4 variegated Cream
5yds 20″ (5 m) of Kacoonda 4mm wide silk ribbon No 4 variegated Cream
1 skein of Kacoonda thick silk No 4 variegated Cream
1 skein of DMC stranded thread No Ecru Cream
1 ball of DMC crochet cotton No 8-Ecru Cream

1 skein of DMC Perle thread No 5-712 Cream, for the cords (or purchase some cream cord or double sided satin ribbon).

Note:

All the silk ribbon is embroidered in a hoop using a No 18 Chenille needle, unless otherwise stated in your instructions. Embroider the fine embroidery out of the hoop.

The glass seed beads should be sewn on using a No 10 Crewel needle and the pearl beads should be sewn on using a No 9 Crewel needle.

Step 1

Hand tack the cotton voile to the back of one of the pieces of silk fabric which you are going to embroider. The tacking should be $1/2$" (1cm) in from the raw edge.

Step 2

Transfer the positions for th Gardenia flowers first. Check Transferring Instructions. Cut three pieces of silk ribbon $19^1/2$" (50cm). Use the 13mm wide silk ribbon No 4 and a No 9 Crewel needle, with one strand of Ecru stranded thread. Check Stitch Guide for the instructions on embroidering the Gardenias. Start your running stitch $1/2$" (1cm) in from the raw edge. Using a knot and an over stitch, embroider a small running stitch in a

Gardenia Flowers

wave along the full length of the ribbon until $1/2$" (1cm) from the end. Do not end this thread off, just leave it hanging. Thread another Crewel No 9 needle with one strand of Ecru stranded thread and anchor this thread in the centre of the position for the Gardenia.

Take a stiletto or knitting needle and poke a hole in the fabric to push the end of the silk ribbon through to the back of the fabric. Using the needle and thread, which is already anchored in your fabric, anchor the end of the silk ribbon which you pushed through to the wrong side. Bring the needle up to the right side and gather the ribbon in a little and start stitching the ribbon, in a snail like manner, in an anti clockwise direction. The stitches will be in the centre of the ribbon and are stab stitches. Try not to lay the ribbon flat on the silk fabric, try to push the ribbon up, so it mounts up on itself. This will give the flower a raised up effect. When you have used all your ribbon, make another hole in the fabric as you did in the beginning and push the ribbon through the fabric and anchor the ribbon off. Embroider the other Gardenias in the same way. Do not worry if one flower ends up larger or smaller than the other, remember not all flowers are the same.

Step 3

Embroider the leaves around the Gardenia, using 4mm wide silk ribbon No 4. Each leaf is one lazy daisy stitch with the holding stitch extended a little longer.

Step 4

Embroider the Daisies, using 4mm wide silk ribbon No 4. Each Daisy has five even petals in lazy daisy stitch and each bud is one lazy daisy stitch. Hand

Small Silk Ribbon Daisy

sew a cream medium pearl bead in the centre of each Daisy. Embroider the Daisy leaves using two strands of Ecru stranded thread and each leaf is one small fly stitch. Embroider around the buds next, using the same thread as the leaves and embroider one fly stitch around each bud extending the holding stitch back to the Daisy to form the stem.

Step 5

Embroider the Forget-me-nots, using the thick silk No 4 and a Chenille No 18 needle. Each set of Forget-me-nots is four colonial knots using the silk thread. The centre of each Forget-me-not is one glass cream seed bead. Use a No 10 Crewel needle to hand sew the glass seed bead in place.

Forget-me-nots

Fine Vine Embroidery

Step 6

Embroider the fine outside embroidery, using one strand of Ecru stranded thread and a No 10 Crewel needle. Embroider one straight stitch at the outside first and then one fly stitch around this straight stitch, extending the holding stitch a little to form the stem.

Hand sew three glass seed beads on the end of each spoke. Each seed bead should be sewn on separately.

Step 7

It is a good idea to initial and date your embroidery.

Making Up Your Evening Bag

Step 1

Embroider four buttonhole eyelets, using two strands of Ecru stranded thread and a No 9 Crewel needle. The eyelet holes are only embroidered at the top of the embroidered section. Carefully poke a hole in the fabric, with a stiletto or knitting needle, where the eyelet hole markings are on your design. Embroider buttonhole stitches all around this hole to form the eyelet.

Step 2

Fold the right sides of the fabric together and machine along the side seam, leaving a $\frac{1}{2}$" (1cm) seam allowance. Sew the embroidered section and the plain section, which is the inside of the bag. You will end up with two separate sections. Place the two top edges of the bag together with the wrong sides facing each other, pin and then hand tack around this edge. Overlock these two edges together. This is the top edge which you crochet around. If you do not crochet, you could hand sew cotton lace around this edge, but crochet does finish the bag off beautifully. Machine two rows of gathering stitches around the bottom

edge of the embroidered section. It is a good idea to overlock this edge before you machine the gathering stitches as this fabric frays. Repeat this step for the gathering for the inside lining.

Step 3

The evening bag stands on four little feet attached to the base of the bag. Do not cut the circle of the base out. See the pattern for the positions of the feet. Each of the feet are made up of one large pearl bead and three small glass seed beads. Take a No 10 Crewel needle and anchor it in one of the feet positions. Bring the needle through to the outside of the silk fabric. Thread the large pearl bead onto the needle as well as three glass seed beads, take the needle back through the pearl bead only and back through the silk fabric, end this thread off securely. Repeat this step for each of the other legs.

Step 4

It is time to assemble the base of the bag. Take the plain piece of silk fabric and place it on a table. Place the template plastic, cut to the circle size, on top of the silk fabric. Place the wadding on top of the template plastic and then the piece of silk which has the pearl bead feet facing outwards on the wadding. Pin and hand tack around the circle of plastic. You will have to centre

the plastic so the four feet are centred. Sew a row of machine stitching around the hand tacking line. Cut the excess fabric away to leave a $1/2''$ (1cm) seam allowance. Overlock this edge now to avoid fraying. Gather the embroidered section to fit around this circle evenly. The best way to achieve even gathering is to divide the embroidered section into quarters and divide the circle into quarters. Place a pin on each marking. Place each quarter marking onto each other and this will give you even gathering all around. Pin the embroidered section to the base and machine a stitch line $1/2''$ (1cm) in from the raw edge.

Gather the lining to fit around the inside of the base and quarter this as well to achieve even gathering. Turn the seam allowance under, and hand sew this lining around, using two strands of Ecru stranded thread and a No 9 Crewel needle.

Step 5

Machine the two stitch lines around the top of the bag (where marked on your pattern) to form the casing for the cords. The eyelet holes should end up in the centre of the casing or machine lines. Make the cords using the Ecru Perle thread No 5 or purchase satin ribbons or cords. If you would like to make your own cords, please refer to

the Stitch Guide on how to make the cords. I have also added a few pearl beads to the ties of the cords for an extra trim. I used a No 10 Crewel needle and one strand of Ecru stranded thread. Thread 1 medium cream pearl bead and three cream glass seed beads onto the strand of thread, take the thread back through the pearl bead only. Take the thread out of the needle and you have two strands hanging, thread both strands into the No 10 Crewel needle and then thread 21 cream glass seed beads onto this thread. I made six of these trimmings. Hand sew the pearl trimmings securely into the knotted cord ends.

Step 6

Now is the time to crochet around the top edge of the evening bag.

1st row: Using the No .60 crochet hook, crochet a double crochet around the top edge. You might find the hook does not like going through the fabric but if you poke a hole in the fabric with a large needle first, it will make it easy for the hook to go through the fabric. This can be a little time consuming but it is well worth it, to crochet this lovely edge.

2nd row: Change to the No 1 hook and crochet another double crochet row on top of the previous row.

3rd row: *1 treble into the next double crochet, four chain, 1 treble into the same double crochet, 4 chain repeat from *.

4th row: *1 long treble into the 4 chain space between the 2 trebles from the previous row, 1 picot of 4 chain, repeat this step 5 more times into the same 4 chain loop. You must have 6 long trebles with a picot in-between each long treble. Then 1 double crochet into the next 4 chain loop which is in-between the 2 trebles, repeat from*. End the threads off securely. Iron the crocheted edge following the instructions from the small pink embroidered Chrysanthemum Lavender bag.

'Miss Angelina'
the Embroidered
Doll Ornament

This beautiful doll, is part of the JW "Collection of Pincushion Dolls". These two dolls, however, are not pincushions — they are ornaments only. I started this collection in 1994 and it is growing all the time. The collection to date has seven wool embroidered dolls and three silk ribbon embroidered dolls but by the time this book is printed there will be more. I love dolls and I love to embroider beautiful dresses for them. My days of dressmaking experience help with the cutting and styling of these dresses. I hope you enjoy embroidering these two beautiful doll ornaments as much as I did. The embroidery on this doll is almost the same colour as the silk fabric, making the embroidery tone on tone. It is best to use a sewing machine for some of this project, but if you do not have one, you could sew it by hand. The dolls are approximately 10″ (25cm) tall when completed.

Requirements:

12″ x 1yd 9″ (30cm x 115cm) of Karachi coloured pure silk dupion

14″ x 1yd 9″ (35cm x 115cm) of cream cotton voile

4″ x 1yd 23″ (10cm x 150cm) of cream tulle

8″ x 8″ square (20cm x 20cm) of pure wool flannel, to cover the film canister

1 half doll especially painted to match the fabric, with holes to sew her on

One set of straight standing legs approx $3^{1}/_{4}$″ (8cm) in height, with holes in the top to sew the legs onto the body of the doll

1 plastic film canister 2″ (5cm) in height, $1^{1}/_{2}$″ (3cm) in diameter, for the body of the doll

Some small rocks or fishing sinkers to weight the film canister

Sewing thread to match the silk fabric

1 packet of DMC glass seed beads No 06-733 Autumn, Antique colours

1 spring hoop 5″ (13cm) in diameter.

Ribbons & Threads:

6yds 21″ (6 m) of Kacoonda silk ribbon 7mm wide No 105 variegated Autumn colours

8yds 28″ (8 m) of Kacoonda 4mm wide silk ribbon No 105 variegated Autumn colours

1 skein of DMC stranded thread No 611 Light Olive Brown

Note:

It is going to be difficult to work in a hoop for all the embroidery on this project. I found I had to embroider some of the silk ribbon embroidery out of the hoop. Try and embroider all the Carnations in the hoop. The lazy daisy flowers can be embroidered out of the hoop. Use a No 18 Chenille needle for the silk ribbon, unless otherwise stated, a No 9 Crewel needle for the fine embroidery and a No 10 Crewel for sewing on the glass seed beads. Only use 12″ (30cm) of silk ribbon at any time, unless otherwise stated in your instructions.

Step 1

Mark the outline of the skirts and train, but do not cut them out. Hand tack the outline of the skirts and train. Hand tack the cotton voile to the back of the silk fabric approx. $^1/_2$″ (1cm) in from the raw edge.

Step 2

Transfer the markings for the Carnations first. Check your Transferring

Carnation

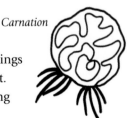

Instructions for details on how to do this. To make the Carnations, cut lengths of 10″ (25cm) of 7mm wide Kacoonda silk ribbon No 105. Take one strand of stranded thread No 611 and a No 9 Crewel needle and anchor your thread into the end of the ribbon (which has been folded over) checking the Stitch Guide for details. You will have to do a couple of overstitches as well when you anchor, then run a small running stitch along the bottom edge of the silk ribbon all the way to the other end, turning the end of the silk ribbon in (as you did when you started). Do not end this thread off. Take another thread the same as you started with and anchor this new thread into the position for the first Carnation. Place the gathered silk ribbon in position and catch it. Gather the silk ribbon up and stitch it onto the fabric, in a snail like direction (you will be stitching the silk ribbon on in an anti clockwise direction). Use very small stab stitches. Repeat this step for all the Carnations.

Step 3

Embroider the leaves around the Carnations, using three strands of stranded thread No 611. Each leaf is, one fly stitch, embroider another fly stitch on top of the first fly stitch, but make the gap narrower this time, embroider one straight stitch in the centre of the last fly stitch. Embroider the remaining leaves in the same manner.

Step 4

Daisy

Transfer the positions for the Daisies. Embroider all the Daisy flowers using 4mm wide silk ribbon No 105. Each Daisy has five even lazy daisy stitch petals. Embroider the buds using the same ribbon and one lazy daisy stitch per bud. The centre of each Daisy is three glass seed beads No 06-733, sewn on separately. Hand sew these beads on using a No 10 Crewel needle.

Step 5

Embroider the Daisy leaves, using two strands of stranded thread No 611. The leaves around the Daisies are one small fly stitch only. Embroider the greenery around each bud using the same thread. Embroider one fly stitch around each bud and extend the holding stitch back to the Daisy.

Step 6

Groups of four Colonial Knots

I have embroidered small groups of four colonial knots, using three strands of stranded thread No 611 These groups of knots are like Forget-me-nots, but they do not have centres.

Step 7

Embroider the fine embroidery, using a No 10 Crewel needle and one strand of stranded thread No 611. Embroider one straight stitch first and then embroider one fly stitch around the straight stitch and extend the holding stitch a little longer to form the stem. Hand sew three glass seed beads No 06-733 on the end of each spoke of the fine embroidery. Each seed bead should be sewn on separately. Check your design carefully when sewing on the glass seed beads, because on the bottom of the front and back skirt there will be some seed beads you will not be able to sew on at this stage, as the sewing machine will hit them. The bottom sections are the ones to watch. You will have to check the train edge as well. These beads can be sewn on once you have made your skirt and train up.

Fine Embroidered Vine

Step 8

It is a good idea to initial and date your embroidery.

How to Assemble Your Beautiful Doll Ornament

Step 1

Cut a circle of woollen flannel fabric 7" (18cm) in diameter. Fill the film canister with small rocks to weight it. Make sure you place the lid of the canister on firmly. Using strong thread (DMC Perle No 5-712 cream thread is very good) run a running stitch around the outside of the circle about $^1/_2$" (1cm) in from the raw edge. Make sure you start with a knot and a couple of overstitches because you will be pulling this thread in tight and if your knot comes out, you will have to start again. When you have embroidered your running stitch all around the circle, pull the thread in a little and then place the film canister inside the woollen circle. Draw the running stitch in until it covers

the canister completely, end this thread off securely. Hand sew the covered canister to the top of the straight porcelain legs. You now have the body and legs for the doll.

Step 2

Cut the tulle into two pieces, 2" x 1yd 23" (5cm x 150cm). Machine two rows of gathering stitches along the top edge $^1/_4$" (5mm) apart. Tie one end of the gathering threads off securely. Take the other set of gathering threads and pull them in to fit around the top section of the body of the doll. When it fits perfectly, tie these threads off as well. Do not cut the threads off as they can be used to hand sew the tulle around the body of the doll. Repeat this step for the second row of tulle. The second row of tulle goes just below the top row, but high enough so you do not see it below the silk embroidered skirt. Hand sew this row of tulle to the bottom section of the body of the doll.

Step 3

Cut the skirts of the doll out now. Cut along the side seam of the skirt allowing $^1/_4$" (5mm) seam allowance. Place both embroidered sections of the skirt with right sides together and pin along the side seam. Machine along the seam allowance. It is a good idea to overlock or oversew the raw edges of the side seams. Do not sew along the top edge. Machine the under skirt the same as the top skirt. Iron the side seams carefully. The seams must be ironed flat.

Place the two right sides of the skirts together at the bottom edge of the skirt. Pin around this line and machine with $^1/_4$" (5mm) seam allowance. Turn the skirts through the top opening, so the embroidery side is facing out. Hand tack the edge around the bottom of the skirt and iron it. Do not remove the tacking thread along the bottom of the skirt at this stage.

Turn the skirt to the wrong side, the wrong side is the lining of the skirt. Using two strands of matching stranded thread, tie a knot in your thread and run a small running stitch through both layers of the silk approx 1" (2cm) down from the top raw edge. You should check the measurement of your skirt to make sure the bottom of the skirt will be covering the shoes of the legs. You might find your doll's measurements vary from mine because your doll's body/film canister is a little larger or smaller than mine. Make sure you start with a knot and a couple of overstitches, but do not end this thread off when you finish your running stitch. Draw the running stitch in as far as you can and then end the thread off. Turn the skirt to the right side and place the skirt over the body and legs of your doll. Secure the skirt to the fabric around the film canister, make sure you catch it well. Place the doll's half body to the top of the skirt and secure the doll in position through the holes in her waist. Make sure you secure the doll firmly to the base of the body using strong thread (dental floss is very good).

Step 4

Cut a piece of bias fabric 2"x 9" (5cm x 23 cm) out of the silk fabric. Fold the fabric with the right side in and machine along the long side $^1/_4$" (5mm) in from the raw edge. Do not stitch across both ends. Push the piece of bias silk fabric through to the right side with a pencil or knitting needle. Turn the open edge in and hand sew across the opening.

Step 5

Fold the bias strip in half to find the centre of the band. Following the instructions on how to make a Carnation, make one Carnation and hand sew it to the centre of the band. It will not be possible to embroider this Carnation in the hoop. Place the piece of bias fabric around the half doll's waist

with the Carnation in the centre front of the skirt. It is a good idea to secure the band at the front of the doll's waist as well as the sides. These catches must not be seen. Fold the ties over each other at the back of the doll's waist and catch in the centre of the band to keep it in place. This band will cover the holes in the doll's waist and also where you have sewn the doll onto the skirt. These dolls are ornaments, so treat them with great care.

'Miss Bernadette' the Embroidered Doll Ornament

This doll is the same embroidery as "Miss Angelina" only the colours are different. Follow the previous doll instructions, using the different coloured ribbons listed below.

Requirements:
12" x 1yd 9" (30cm x 115cm) of black pure silk dupion
14" x 1yd 9" (35cm x 115cm) of cream cotton voile
4" x 1yd 23" (10cm x 150cm) of cream tulle
8" x 8" (20cm x 20cm) of pure wool flannel to cover

the film canister
1 half doll especially painted to match the fabric, with holes to sew her on One set of straight standing legs, approx $3^1/_2$" (8cm) in height, with holes in the top to sew the legs onto the body of the doll
1 plastic film canister 2" (5cm) in height, $1^1/_2$" (3cm) in diameter, for the body of the doll
Some small rocks or fishing sinkers to

weight the film canister
Sewing thread to match the silk fabric
1 packet of Mill Hill glass seed beads No
030334 Deep Maroon
1 spring hoop 5″ (13cm) in diameter.

Ribbons & Threads:
3 cards of Bucilla silk ribbon 7mm wide
variegated No 2-7115 Burgundies
4 cards of Bucilla silk ribbon 4mm wide
No 042 Maroon
1 skein of DMC stranded cotton No 814
Dark Maroon, No 3011 Medium Green.

Follow the instructions for Miss Angelina
taking care to substitute the correct
colours.

The Sunflower
Blooms in the Garden

This is a good way to enter into silk ribbon embroidery. If you do not want to frame this piece you could make it into a small cushion or Lavender bag. I have given you the fabric measurements for a framing only.

Requirements:

1 piece of cream Olympia linen Ecru
$10^1/_2$″ x $10^1/_2$″ (27cm x 27cm)
1 piece of cream cotton voile 12″ x 12″
(30cm x 30cm)
Needles: Chenille No 18 and Crewel No 9
1 spring hoop 5″ or 7″ (13cm or 18cm) in diameter.

Ribbons & Threads:

1 card of 7mm wide Bucilla silk ribbon
No 7105 Daffodils variegated
1 card of the following Bucilla silk ribbon
4mm wide- No 501 Off White, No 502
Banana, No 459 Very Light Blue, No 009
Lilac, No 544 Light Pink, No 656 Lemon
Yellow
DMC stranded thread No 522 Green, No
712 Cream. Small amounts of the
following numbers, No 780 Rust, No 800
Blue, No 744 Yellow, No 745 Banana.

Note:

When embroidering with silk ribbon, you should embroider in a hoop. I do not embroider my fine stranded embroidery in the hoop. Do not tie knots in your ribbon. Secure your starting and finishing ribbon with one thread of cream stranded thread and use a No 9 Crewel needle. All silk ribbon embroidery in this project should be embroidered using a No 18 Chenille needle. Mark your design with a water-soluble pen which can be removed with cold water.

Step 1

Hand tack the cotton voile to the back side of the linen fabric using a small running stitch approx. $^1/_2$″ (1cm) in from the raw edge.

Step 2

Transfer your design. Following the Transferring Instructions. It is very simple if you follow the instructions I have given you.

Step 3

Embroider a tight circle of colonial knots using six strands of stranded cotton No 780.

Cut 12" (30cm) of 7mm wide silk ribbon No 7105 and using the No 18 Chenille needle, embroider the Sunflower. Each petal of the Sunflower is one ribbon stitch. Embroider the petals in the numbered order, this will make it easy to evenly position your petals. Embroider one small straight stitch in the centre of each petal at the base of the ribbon stitch petal using one strand of stranded thread No 744. This stitch will make your ribbon stitch a little more secure.

Sunflower

Stem and Leaves

Step 4

Embroider the stem of the Sunflower and the bud, using stem stitch and two strands of stranded thread No 522. Embroider the leaves next using the same thread. Each leaf is one lazy daisy stitch with the holding stitch extended a little longer. Embroider one straight stitch in the centre of each leaf using the same thread.

Sunflower Bud

Stem and Leaves

Step 5

Embroider the Sunflower bud. Embroider two ribbon stitches in the shape of a V and then embroider another in between the first two stitches.

Embroider one small straight stitch in the centre of each bud petal using one strand of stranded thread No 744. Embroider one fly stitch around the bud using two strands of stranded thread No 522. Embroider another fly stitch around the previous fly stitch.

Step 6

Embroider the blue flower stems, using two strands of stranded thread No 522 and continuous fly stitch. Make sure you start from the outside and work in. Start with one straight stitch and then begin the continuous fly stitch.

Embroider the banana coloured stems in the same manner.

Step 7

Embroider the blue flowers, using 4mm wide silk ribbon No 459 and embroider five even ribbon stitch petals per flower. Make sure you are very careful with the ribbon stitch as the curl on the end will pull through the fabric, if you are too heavy handed. Embroider one small straight stitch in the centre of each petal at the base of each ribbon stitch using one strand of stranded thread No 800. Embroider the centre of each flower using 4mm wide silk ribbon No 656 and one colonial knot. The buds are one ribbon stitch in the same ribbon as the flowers, with a small straight stitch in the centre

Blue Ribbobn Stitch Bud and Leaves

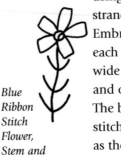

Blue Ribbon Stitch Flower, Stem and Leaves

of each ribbon stitch (as in the flowers).

Repeat this same flower and bud for the banana coloured 4mm wide silk ribbon No 502. Embroider the straight stitch using one strand of stranded thread No 745. The centre of the flower is the same as the blue flowers.

Yellow Ribbon Stitch Bud, Stem and Leaves

Yellow Ribbon Stitch Flower, Stem and Leaves

Step 8

Embroider the cream Daisy, using 4mm wide silk ribbon No 501. Embroider five even lazy daisy petals for the Daisy and embroider one lazy daisy stitch for each bud. Embroider the leaves of the Daisy next, using two strands of stranded thread No 522. Each leaf is one lazy daisy stitch with the holding stitch extended a little longer. Embroider one fly stitch around each bud using the same thread

Daisy and Buds

Step 9

Embroider the stems of the mauve flowers, using two strands of stranded thread No 522 and feather stitch. You must start at the outside of the stem

and work in with this stitch. Embroider the mauve flowers using 4mm wide silk ribbon No 009 and one colonial knot per flower.

Feather Stitch Stems with Mauve Flowers

Step 10

Embroider the Tulip stem, using two strands of stranded thread No 522. Each stem is stitched using one straight stitch at the top and then one fly stitch around the straight stitch extending the holding stitch to form the Tulips. Embroider the tulip flowers, using 4mm wide silk ribbon No 544 and one colonial knot for each Tulip flower.

Tulips

Step 11

Embroider the Forget-me-knots, using 4mm wide silk ribbon No 459. Embroider four outside colonial knots very close together. Embroider another colonial knot in the centre of the four outside colonial knots, using 4mm silk ribbon No 656.

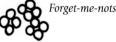 *Forget-me-nots*

Step 12

It is a good idea to initial and date your embroidery. Have your embroidery framed in your choice of frame. You should have your work framed by a professional who is experienced in embroidery framing.

The Ruby Rose Garden
Framing

This small embroidery is a very simple project and is great for someone who has never embroidered with silk ribbon before. You might wish to make a very small cushion or Lavender bag instead of a framing, but I have only given you the fabric for a framing.

Requirements:
1 piece of cream Olympia linen $10^1/_2$" x $10^1/_2$" (27cm x 27cm)
1 piece of cream cotton voile 12" x 12" (30cm x 30cm)
1 spring hoop 5" or 7" (13cm or 18cm) in diameter
Needles: No 18 Chenille and No 9 Crewel.

Ribbons & Threads:
1 card of Bucilla silk ribbon No 1306 Burgundies variegated
1 card each of the following 4mm wide Bucilla silk ribbon No 459 Very Light Blue, No 042 Maroon, No 656 Lemon Yellow, No 501 Off White, No 544 Light Pink
1 skein each of the following DMC stranded threads No 522 Green and No 712 Cream, small amounts of the following colours No 800 Blue, No 310 Black, No 744 Yellow, No 815 Maroon
2 threads of DMC Perle thread No 5-712 Cream.

Note:
Make sure you embroider the silk ribbon embroidery in a hoop and I embroider the stranded thread embroidery out of the hoop. The silk ribbon embroidery is worked using a Chenille No 18 needle and the fine embroidery using a No 9 Crewel needle. As a rule, only use 12" (30cm) pieces of ribbon when embroidering with silk ribbon. Some designs might require more ribbon, so read your instructions carefully.

Step 1

Hand tack the cotton voile to the back of the cream linen approx. $^1/_2{}''$ (1cm) in from the raw edge.

Step 2

Transfer your design as per the Transferring Instructions. Only transfer a small amount at any one time.

Step 3

The first flower you will embroider is the large Rose in the centre.

Cut 12" (30cm) of the 13mm wide silk ribbon No 1306. Thread your Crewel No 9 needle with one strand of stranded thread No 815. Please check your Stitch Guide for instructions on making this Rose.

Rose Stem and Leaves

How to Embroider the Gathered Rose or Carnation:

These flowers can vary depending on the particular project you are working on. Sometimes you will use 7mm wide silk ribbon and other times you will use 13mm wide silk ribbon. The length of silk ribbon will also vary, so please read your instructions carefully.

Cut the required length of silk ribbon which will be in the instructions for the particular project you are embroidering.

Step 1

Embroider the stem of the Rose using two strands of stranded thread No 522 and stem stitch. Embroider the leaves next using the same thread. The leaves are one lazy daisy stitch with the holding stitch extended a little longer.

Daisy on a Stem

Step 2

Embroider the cream Daisy flowers first, before the stems, as it is easier to place the stem once the flower has been embroidered. The Daisy flowers are five even lazy daisy petals, using 4mm wide silk ribbon No 501. The centres of the Daisies are one colonial knot using 4mm wide silk ribbon No 656.

Embroider the Daisy stems next, using two strands of stranded thread No 522 and continuous fly stitch. Make sure you start the continuous fly stitch stem from the Daisy.

Step 3

Embroider the feather stitch vine, using two strands of stranded thread No 522 and feather stitch. Start to embroider these stems from the outside in.

Feather Stitch Vine

Embroider one colonial knot on the end of each spoke using 4mm wide silk ribbon No 042.

Ribbon Stitch Flowers

Bee

Step 4

Embroider the blue ribbon stitch flowers, using 4mm wide silk ribbon No 459. Each flower has five even petals. Embroider one small straight stitch in the centre of the ribbon stitch at the base of the petal with one strand of stranded thread No 800.

Embroider one colonial knot in the centre of each flower using, 4mm wide silk ribbon No 656.

Tulips

Step 5

Embroider the stems of the Tulips, using two strands of stranded thread No 522. Embroider one straight stitch at the top first and then one fly stitch around the straight stitch. Extend the holding stitch to form the stem of the Tulip. Embroider the Tulip flower, using 4mm wide silk ribbon No 544 and one colonial knot.

Step 6

Embroider the bee. Embroider the body of the bee, using three strands of stranded thread No 744 and very close satin stitch.

Embroider the bee's stripes next, using two strands of stranded thread No 310. Embroider a small fly stitch around the bee's bottom first and extend the holding stitch to form the bee's sting.

Embroider the first stripe (which is a small straight stitch) across the fly stitch

and then another stripe at the front end of the bee and one in the middle.

Embroider the bee's eyes next, using the same thread. The eyes, at the front end of the bee's body, are two colonial knots very close together. Embroider the feelers next using two straight stitches between the eyes in the same thread. It is best to stitch the feelers from the outside in.

Embroider the bee's legs using the same thread and straight stitches for the long section of the leg and a smaller straight stitch for the bend of the leg.

Embroider the bee's wings next, using Perle thread No 5-712. I use the Chenille No 18 needle for my bullions, but you might choose to use another needle. Embroider the bee's wings using bullion stitch and fifteen twists for each wing.

You might have to adjust the number of twists according to your tension. I have a very tight tension with my bullion stitches. The bee has four wings, two on each side of the body. Check bee instructions for diagrams.

Step 7

It is a good idea to initial and date your embroidery.

You could choose to frame this project or make it into a small cushion or Lavender bag. The choice is yours, but the material given is for the framed version only.

The Hollyhock Garden
Framing

This project is small and quick to embroider for first time embroiderers.

A very simple project, but one of my favourites. You might wish to make this project into a cushion, framing or Lavender bag. I love embroidering on this coloured linen.

Requirements:
1 piece of Oatmeal Belfast linen 10″ x 10″ (25cm x 25cm)
1 piece of cream cotton voile 12″ x 12″ (30cm x 30cm)
1 spring hoop 5″ or 7″ (13cm or 18cm) in diameter
Needles: No 18 Chenille and No 9 Crewel.

Ribbons and Threads:
1 card of Bucilla 7mm wide silk ribbon No 7106 Purple Haze variegated
1 card of Bucilla 4mm wide silk ribbon No 042 Maroon, No 656 Lemon Yellow, No 532 Salmon
1 skein of DMC stranded thread No 522 Green, No 712 Cream.

Note:
Embroider all silk ribbon using the No 18 Chenille and only use 12″ (30cm) of silk ribbon at a time. Always embroider the silk ribbon in a hoop but fine embroidery can be embroidered without a hoop.

Step 1
Hand tack the cotton voile to the backside of the linen using a small running stitch approx. $1/2″$ (1cm) in from the raw edge.

Step 2
Transfer your design as per Transferring Instructions. Only transfer a small section at a time.

Step 3
Embroider the centre Hollyhock first, using 7mm wide silk ribbon No 7106. These flowers are embroidered using a French knot, but you will twist the ribbon

around the needle three times (very loosely). You can tighten your tension as the flower reaches the top, but keep the bottom section very loose.

Embroider the leaves next, using two strands of stranded thread No 522. Each leaf is one lazy daisy stitch with the holding stitch slightly extended.

Step 4

Embroider the Daisies, using 4mm wide silk ribbon No 042. Each Daisy has five even petals and each bud has one lazy daisy stitch. Embroider the Daisy stem next, using two strands of stranded thread No 522 and continuous fly stitch starting from the Daisy. Embroider one fly stitch around each bud and extend the holding stitch back to the Daisy to form the bud stem using the same thread. Embroider one small fly stitch leaf on each Daisy using the same thread. Embroider the Daisy centre next using 4mm wide silk

*Daisy Buds,
Leaves and
Stems*

ribbon No 656 and one colonial knot.

Step 5

Embroider the vine, using two strands of stranded thread No 522 and feather stitch. You must start the feather stitch from the outside and work in. Embroider the flowers on the vine using 4mm wide silk ribbon No 532 and one colonial knot on the end of each spoke of the feather stitch.

*Feather
Stitch
Vine*

Step 6

Embroider the Tulip stems, using two strands of stranded thread No 522. Embroider one straight stitch at the top and then one fly stitch around the straight stitch and extend the holding stitch a little longer to form the stem of the Tulip. Embroider one colonial knot on the top of the stem to form the flower, using 4mm wide silk ribbon No 042.

Tulips

Step 7

It is a good idea to initial and date your embroidery. Have your embroidery framed or make a small cushion or Lavender bag, the choice is yours.

Illustration only

The Sunflower
and Watering Can Cushion

This beautiful cushion will look great in any room. If you have not embroidered with silk ribbon before, this might be a good "second" project. I think you need to have at least tried silk ribbon embroidery before attempting this project. It is not difficult, but a little experience is necessary.

Requirements:
1 piece of Oatmeal Belfast linen 15″ x 15″ (38cm x 38cm)
28″ (70cm) of silk fabric to match your linen
1 piece of cream cotton voile 16″ x 16″ (40cm x 40cm)
10″ (25cm) fawn zip
A cushion insert to fit your finished cushion, remember your insert should be larger than your cushion to make your cushion very firm and full. I usually make my own cushion inserts.
1 spring hoop 7″ (18cm) in diameter
Needles: No 18 Chenille, No 9 & 7 Crewel.

Ribbons and Threads:
3 cards of Bucilla silk ribbon 7mm wide No 7105 Daffodils variegated
2 cards of Bucilla silk ribbon 7mm wide No 501 Cream
1 card of Bucilla silk ribbon 4mm wide No 322 Robin Egg, No 656 Lemon Yellow
1 skein of DMC stranded thread No 522 Green, No 780 Rust, No 744 Yellow, No 712 Cream, a small amount of No 310 Black
1 skein of DMC Perle thread No 5-842 Fawn, No 5-5282 Gold, No 5-712 Cream
1 skein of DMC Perle thread No 3-842 Fawn
A small amount of DMC glitter thread No Art 272 Blanc.

Make sure all silk ribbon embroidery is embroidered in the hoop. I embroider my stranded thread embroidery out of the hoop. I use a spring hoop as it does not damage the silk ribbon. When embroidering a larger project such as this cushion, you will have to at some stage place the hoop over your previous embroidery. I use No 18 Chenille needles for all the silk ribbon and No 9 & 7 Crewel needles for my stranded embroidery.

Step 1

Hand tack the cotton voile to the back side of the linen fabric using a small running stitch about $\frac{1}{2}''$ (1cm) in from the raw edge.

Step 2

Transfer your design as per transfer instructions. Only transfer a small section at a time.

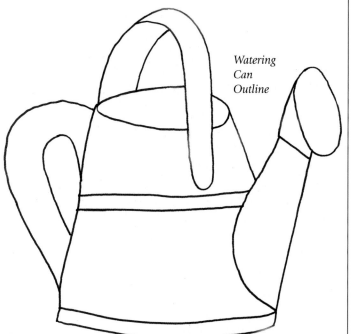

Watering Can Outline

Step 3

Make sure you use the correct thickness of thread for the watering can. The outline is embroidered using the thin thread and the whipping is embroidered in the thick thread. Embroider the outline of the watering can first, using Perle thread No 5-842 and chain stitch the outline of the watering can. Some of the watering can might be covered with flowers, but you must embroider the whole outline. Whip the chain outline using Perle thread No 3-842. Remember when you are whipping, your thread must be long enough to whip the entire section being whipped, as you cannot join the whipping. Embroider the holes in the watering can spout using Perle thread No 3-842 and embroider one colonial knot for each hole. Embroider the dots around the two bands on the watering can using Perle thread No 5-5282 gold metallic and one colonial knot per dot. Embroider the two screws on the watering can's handle using the same thread and colonial knots for each screw.

Embroidery on Watering Can

Step 4

Embroider the floral design on the lower area of the watering can, using Perle thread No 5-842. Embroider the Daisies first, using five evenly placed lazy daisy stitches for each Daisy. Embroider the leaves around the Daisies using the same thread. Each leaf is one fly stitch. Embroider the centres of the Daisies using the same thread and embroider one colonial for each centre of each Daisy. Embroider the feather stitch vine next, using the same thread. Start your feather stitch from the outside and embroider in. Embroider the Forget-me-nots next, using the same thread. Each Forget-me-not has four outside knots. These knots are colonial knots. The centre knot is one

colonial knot embroidered using Perle thread No 5-5282 gold.

Step 5

Embroider the Sunflowers. A helpful hint when embroidering the Sunflowers: To ensure your petals are even, draw a circle the size of the flower first and make sure your petals do not go outside this line. Embroider the centre of the Sunflower first, using six strands of stranded thread No 780. The centre must be a very tight circle of colonial knots. I use a No 18 Chenille needle for the knots.

Embroider the Sunflower petals next, following the Sunflower diagram. The petals of the Sunflower are embroidered using 7mm wide silk ribbon No 7105 and ribbon stitches. The ribbon stitch petals start from the outside circle of the centre of the Sunflower. Embroider one small straight stitch in the centre of each petal at the base of the petal, using a single strand of stranded thread No 744.

Sunflower

Leaves

Half a Sunflower

Step 6

Embroider the Sunflower buds. Embroider the centre of the buds first, using six strands of stranded thread No 780 and colonial knots.

Embroider the bud petals next in the same manner as the Sunflowers. You can draw a half circle as a guide for the petals, if you wish.

Step 7

Embroider the stems on the Sunflowers and the buds, using two strands of stranded thread No 522 and stem stitch. Embroider the Sunflower leaves next using six strands of stranded thread No 522 and large lazy daisy stitches for each leaf. Extend the holding stitch a little longer on each leaf. Embroider one straight stitch in the centre of each lazy daisy stitch leaf.

Step 8

Embroider the cream Daisies, using 7mm wide silk ribbon No 501. Each Daisy has five even lazy daisy stitch petals. Each Daisy bud has one lazy daisy stitch petal. Embroider the centre of the Daisy, using 4mm wide silk ribbon No 656 and one colonial knot. Embroider the Daisy leaves next, using three strands of stranded thread No 522. Do not extend the holding stitch on these leaves.

Embroider the greenery around each bud using the same thread. Each bud has one fly stitch around each petal with the holding stitch extended back to the Daisy to form the stem of the bud.

Daisy Bud

Dasiy and Leaves

Step 9

Embroider the blue Forget-me-nots, using 4mm wide silk ribbon No 322. The four outside knots are colonial knots.

Forget-me-nots

Embroider the centre of the Forget-me-not using 4mm wide silk ribbon No 656 and one colonial knot.

Step 10

Embroider the bees. First, the bee's body using three strands of stranded thread No 744 and very close satin stitch. Embroider one small fly stitch at the back of the body and extend the holding stitch a little to form the bee's sting, using two strands of stranded thread No 310. Embroider the bee's stripes next, using the same thread. Embroider the first stripe where you started the fly stitch and then the second stripe is near the front of the body. The third stripe is in the middle of the first and second stripe. Embroider the eyes next, using the same thread. Embroider two colonial knots very close together to form the eyes. Embroider the feelers next, using the same thread. The feelers are two straight stitches in the shape of a V from in-between the eyes. The best way to embroider the feelers is to start from the outside and take the needle in-between the eyes. Embroider the legs next, using the same thread. Each leg has one long straight stitch and one short straight stitch for the bend in the leg. Embroider the bee's wings next, using Perle thread No 5-712. Each wing has one bullion stitch with fifteen twists. You might have to

Bee

adjust the number of bullions according to your tension. My bullion tension is very tight. Each bee has four wings, two on each side. Complete the other bees in the same manner.

Step 11

Embroider the water drops from the watering can spout, using glitter thread No Art.272 Blanc. Each water drop is one lazy daisy stitch with the holding stitch extended a little longer. Embroider one straight stitch in the centre of each lazy daisy stitch.

Water

Step 12

It is a good idea to initial and date your embroidery.

How to Make Up Your Cushion

Note:

It is a good idea to slightly round the corners of the cushion as it is much easier to attach the frill. Cut the excess cotton voile away now. If you are using silk fabric for the frill, it is a good idea to overlock the raw edge before you start gathering it up. Silk fabric tends to fray very easily. If you do not machine sew, it is a good idea to get someone, who has had experience in making cushions, to make up your cushion. You have embroidered your cushion beautifully so do not spoil it now.

Step 1

Cut three lengths of silk fabric 6″ x 1yd 9″ (15cm x 115cm) approx. Join the three pieces together to form a circle using $1/2$″ (1 cm) approx. seam allowances.

Iron the seam open with the iron. Turn the fabric to the right side and fold the two raw edges together. Using the iron, press a fold line along the long side of the fabric. Now is a good time to overlock the raw edge to avoid fraying. Machine one row of gathering threads $1/4$″ (5mm) in from the raw edge and then another row of gathering threads $1/4$″ (5mm) from the first row of gathering thread. Divide the frill into quarters and mark each quarter with a pin. Quarter the embroidered section of the top cushion and mark with a pin. Gather the frill up to fit each quarter of the embroidered top cushion and pin in place. If you quarter the frill and the cushion top, your frill will be evenly gathered. Machine the frill onto the embroidered cushion $3/8$″ (5mm) in from the edge. I usually leave the pins in while I sew the frill on as the pins keep the frill firmly in place.

Step 2

Cut two pieces of silk $8^1/2$″ x 15″ (21.5cm x 38cm). Place the two long edges together and machine a seam of 1″ (2.5cm) from the raw edges, making sure you leave a 10″ (25cm) opening in the centre for the zipper. Machine the zipper in next. Open the zipper about 3″ (7.5cm). It is very important to open the zipper at this stage, you will see why soon.

Step 3

Lay the embroidered section on the table with the right side facing up. Lay the right side of the back section onto the right side of the embroidered section and pin both pieces together around the outside. Turn the cushion over, so you can see the machine stitch line where you sewed the frill onto the embroidered section. Machine a line of stitching around this stitch line through both pieces of fabric as well as the frill. Once you have sewn this stitch line, cut any excess fabric away from the edges. Now is the time you use the opening of the zip. Through the opening of the zip, pull the cushion to the right side. If the second row of gathering stitches is showing on your cushion frill, take it out now. Make or buy a cushion insert. I usually make my own inserts as I do not think bought inserts have enough filling in them and you may find it difficult to find the same size to fit your cushion. Always remember the cushion insert should be larger than your embroidered cushion. The insert should be approx 1″ (2.5cm) all the way round larger than your cushion.

A Beautiful Spray of
Apricot Carnations Cushion

This cushion is very elegant, but quite simple if you have embroidered with silk ribbon before. If you have never embroidered with silk ribbon, practice before trying this cushion. Do not be put off by this design, it is not difficult once you have had a small amount of experience. If you do not machine sew, please have your cushion made up by an experienced sewer. The finished size of this cushion without the frill is 11″ square (28cm).

Requirements:
1 piece of cream silk dupion fabric 24″ x 1yd 9″ (60cm x 115cm)
1 piece of cream cotton voile 14″ x 14″ (35cm x 35cm)
8″ (20cm) cream zip
1 spring hoop 7″ (18cm) in diameter
Needles: Chenille No 18 & Crewel No 9.

Ribbons and Threads:
1 card of Bucilla silk ribbon 13mm wide No 1308 Ice Cream variegated
1 card each of 4mm wide silk ribbon No 633 Pale Hunter, No 502 Banana, No 531 Light Coral, No 459 Very Light Blue, No 656 Lemon Yellow
1 skein of DMC stranded thread No 3053 Pale Green, No 712 Cream
A small amount of No 754 Pale Coral, No 744 Yellow.

Note:
Make sure you embroider all silk ribbon using a No 18 Chenille, unless otherwise stated in your instructions, and No 9 Crewel needle for all fine embroidery. When embroidering with silk ribbon make sure you have your fabric in a hoop. Fine embroidery can be embroidered out of the hoop. The Carnations in this spray of flowers are embroidered using a No 9 Crewel needle as these flowers are sitting on the top of the fabric.

Step 1

Hand tack the cotton voile to the back side of the silk fabric, using a small running stitch $^1/_2$″ (1cm) in from the raw edge. It would be a good idea to overlock or oversew the raw edges now as the silk tends to fray when you are embroidering.

Step 2

Transfer your design as per Transferring Instructions and only transfer a small section at any one time.

Step 3

Take the 13mm wide silk ribbon No 1308 and divide the ribbon into five even pieces. The ribbon will be approximately 11″ (28cm) in length, but please check this measurement before you cut the silk ribbon. Using one strand of stranded thread No 712 and a No 9 Crewel needle, make the Carnations up following the instructions for Roses or Carnations in your Stitch Guide. Use only the amount of ribbon mentioned in these instructions, as the Stitch Guide will give you a general measurement. I have chosen the cream stranded thread for the Carnations, as it matches the variegated ribbon much better than the pale coral thread. Hand sew all the Carnations in the correct positions, as per your design sheet.

Carnation Flower

Step 4

Embroider the Carnation leaves, using 4mm wide silk ribbon No 633. Each Carnation has a group of loop stitch leaves, but one has two sets. Check your design for the number of leaves. Bring your needle up near the Carnation and embroider three loop stitch leaves very close together. End each set of leaves off as you go because you can easily pull the

loops tight. It is a good idea to hand sew a small straight stitch at the base of the leaf, using one strand of stranded thread No 3053, so the loop does not pull through.

Step 5

Embroider the coral ribbon stitch flowers, using 4mm wide silk ribbon No 531. Each flower has five even ribbon stitch petals. Make sure you do not pull the loop tight. It is a good idea to embroider a small straight stitch in the centre of each petal at the base of the petal using one strand of stranded thread No 754. Embroider the ribbon stitch flower leaves next, using one strand of stranded thread No 3053. Each leaf has one small fly stitch. Embroider the centres of the flowers, using three strands of stranded thread No 744 and one colonial knot.

Ribbon Stitch Flowers

Step 6

Embroider the stems of the Carnations, using two strands of stranded thread No 3053 and stem stitch. If you embroider the stem stitch starting from the base of the Carnation and working out, then you must embroider all stems in the same direction.

Stems

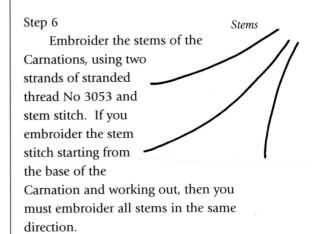

Step 7

Embroider the feather stitch vines, using two strands of stranded thread No

3053 and feather stitch. When embroidering feather stitch, you must start from the outside and embroider in. Embroider the flowers on the feather stitch vine, using 4mm wide silk ribbon No 502 and one colonial knot for each flower.

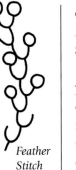

Feather Stitch Vine

Step 8

Embroider the Forget-me-nots, using 4mm wide silk ribbon No 459. Each Forget-me-not has four outside knots very close together and the centre knot is embroidered using 4mm wide silk ribbon No 656. All knots are colonial knots.

Step 9

It is a good idea to initial and date your embroidery. Now, make your cushion up, following the instructions for making up the Sunflower and Watering Can cushion. Note: The frill on this cushion has only two lengths of silk fabric 6″ x 1yd 9″ (15cm x 115cm). The zip is shorter, so only leave an 8″ (20cm) opening in the centre seam. The two back sections are also a different size 12″ x 7″ (30cm x 18cm).

The Wedding Ring Cushion

This cushion is very elegant and would make a beautiful bed cushion after the wedding. It is not a good idea to use the real gold rings on the cushion as many a ring has been lost before it reaches the church. In most cases the cushion is carried by a child and it is a very big responsibility for a child, so please use imitation rings. It is a nice idea to embroider the initials of the bride and groom, the date and the year of the wedding. This will become a lovely momento of the big day. It is also a good idea because some people tend to forget anniversaries very quickly. The finished size of this cushion without the frill is 11″ x 11″ (28cm x 28cm).

Requirements:
1 piece of cream good quality satin 12″ x 45″ (60cm x 115cm)
1 piece of cream cotton voile or 13″ x 13″ (33cm x 33cm)
2 gold wedding rings, plastic
1 string of small cream pearl beads
1 spring hoop 7″ (18cm) in diameter
1 cream zip 8″ (20cm)
Needles: Chenille No 18 & Crewel No 9.

Ribbons and Threads:
2 cards of Bucilla silk ribbon 13mm wide No 1321 Ivory
3 cards of Bucilla silk ribbon 4mm wide No 501 Off White
1 skein of DMC stranded thread No Ecru.

Note:
All silk ribbon embroidery is embroidered in a hoop. Use a No 18 Chenille needle for all silk ribbon embroidery, unless otherwise stated in the instructions. The Carnations in this project are embroidered using a No 9 Crewel needle. Only use 12″ (30cm) of silk ribbon at any time. It is very important to read your instructions carefully.

Step 1
Hand tack the cotton voile to the back side of the satin fabric, $^1/_2$″ (1cm) in from the raw edge. As satin tends to fray when you are embroidering, it would be a good idea to overlock or oversew the raw edges now before you start your embroidery.

Step 2

Transfer your design as per Transferring Instructions. Only transfer a small section at a time.

Step 3

Embroider the heart outline and feather sprays first using two strands of Ecru stranded thread. The heart outline is feather stitch and you must remember to reverse the feather stitch when you get half way around your heart. Embroider the feather stitch vines next, using the same thread and feather stitch. The vines must be embroidered from the outside in.

Step 4

Embroider the Carnations, using 14″ (35cm) of 13mm wide silk ribbon No 1321. Embroider the running stitch along the 13mm wide silk ribbon using one strand of Ecru stranded thread and a No 9 Crewel needle. Follow the Carnation or Rose instructions in the Stitch Guide. Embroider all the Carnations now.

Step 5

Embroider the Carnation leaves, using three strands of Ecru stranded thread. Each set of leaves has three lazy daisy stitches with the holding stitch extended a little.

Step 6

Embroider the lazy daisy flowers and buds, using 4mm wide silk ribbon No 501. Each Daisy has five even petals and one lazy daisy stitch for each petal. Each bud is one lazy daisy stitch. Embroider the Daisy leaves next using two strands of Ecru stranded thread. Each leaf is one small fly stitch. Embroider one fly stitch around the bud, but do not extend the holding stitch. Embroider another fly stitch around the previous fly stitch and extend the holding stitch back to the Daisy to form the stem. Hand sew one small cream bead in the centre of each Daisy with two strands of Ecru stranded thread and a No 9 Crewel needle. Embroider all the Daisies and buds in this manner.

Step 7

Cut two lengths 19$\frac{1}{2}$″ (50cm) of silk ribbon 4mm wide No 501. These will form the bows to hold the rings onto the cushion. Fold the ribbon in half and hand sew the ribbon to the cushion with a couple of overstitches at the end of the featherstitch vine. Take a No 9 Crewel needle and thread it with one strand of Ecru stranded thread. Turn the raw end of the ribbon over and embroider a couple of overstitches into the end of the ribbon. Embroider a small running stitch up the centre of the silk ribbon for about 3″ (8cm) and then draw the gathering stitch up tight so the silk ribbon will end up ruffled on the end. Take the needle back through the ruffle and end the thread off. Repeat this for all the bow ends. Place the plastic ring on the ribbon and tie the silk ribbon in a small bow. It is a good idea to stitch the bow in the centre, so the bow does not come untied.

Step 8

Initial and date your embroidery now. Make your cushion up following the instructions for the Watering Can and Sunflower Cushion. Note: The frill will only have two lengths of satin fabric 6″ x 1yd 9″ (15cm x 115cm). I would suggest you overlock this edge before you machine your gathering threads as this fabric tends to fray when you are pulling up your gathering. The back of the cushion measurements are the same as the Spray of Carnations Cushion. This cushion and the Spray of Carnations Cushion are the same size.

The Wedding Dress Coathanger

This coathanger makes a lovely gift for the bride and matches the ring cushion. The bride's wedding gown will look perfect hanging on this beautiful coathanger.

Requirements:
1 piece of cream satin fabric 8″ x 1yd 9″ (20cm x 115cm)
1 piece of cream cotton voile 8″ x 18″ (20cm x 45cm)
1yd 4″ (1 m) of cream pre-gathered lace 2″ (5mm) wide
1yd 4″ (1 m) of cream beading $1/2$″ (1cm) wide
1yd 4″ (1 m) of cream double sided satin ribbon
1 adult size wooden coathanger
1 piece of wadding 3″ x 1yd 29″ (8cm x 150cm)
1 piece of satin tubing for the hook of the hanger
A small amount of small cream pearl beads
1 spring hoop 5″ (13cm) in diameter
Needles: Chenille No 18 & Crewel No 9
1 gold plastic wedding ring.

Ribbons and Threads:
1 card of Bucilla silk ribbon 13mm wide No 1321 Ivory
2 cards of Bucilla silk ribbon 4mm wide No 501 Off White
1 skein of Ecru DMC stranded thread.

Note:
All silk ribbon is embroidered using a hoop and a No 18 Chenille needle, unless otherwise stated in your instructions.

Step 1

Cut the coathanger shape out following the pattern. Hand tack the cotton voile to the back of the satin fabric. It is a good idea to overlock the raw edges before you embroider. You will only be hand tacking the voile to the embroidered section of the coathanger. Take the pre-gathered lace and the beading and machine the beading lace to the top of the pre-gathered lace, making sure you cover the binding on the pre-gathered lace. Machine the pre-gathered lace and the beading to the bottom of the coathanger

on the bottom of the plain back section and the front embroidered section. Do not thread the 3mm wide ribbon through the beading yet.

Step 2

Transfer the design as per Transferring Instructions. Only transfer a small amount at a time.

Feather Stitch Vine

Step 3

Embroider the heart and vine first, following the same instructions as for the Wedding Cushion.

Step 4

Embroider the Carnations and leaves following the same instructions as for the Wedding Cushion.

Silk Ribbon Bow

Step 5

Embroider the Daisies, Daisy buds and the leaves following the instructions from the Wedding Cushion.

Step 6

Make the bow the same as the Wedding Cushion.

Step 7

Initial and date your embroidery now.

Step 8

Thread the 3mm wide satin ribbon through the beading lace and secure the

ribbon at each end of the coathanger section.

How to Make Up the Wedding Dress Coathanger

Step 1

Screw the hook into the wooden coathanger first. It is very difficult to screw the hook in once the wadding is secure around the coathanger.

Cut the wadding into two strips 3″ wide (7.5cm), and bind the wooden coathanger with the wadding. It is a good idea to secure the starting end and the finishing end of the wadding with a couple of overstitches, using two strands of stranded thread and a No.9 Crewel needle. The wadding forms the padding for the coathanger.

Step 2

Push the satin tubing over the metal hook and secure it, at the base, hook with a couple of overstitches (using the same thread used for securing the wadding). Cut the satin tubing a little longer than the hook and turn the raw end in. Oversew the satin tubing with the same thread.

Step 3

Machine the beading to the top edge of the pre-gathered lace. Overlock the bottom edges, front and back. Machine the pre-gathered lace, with the beading on it, along the lower edge of the right side of the coathanger (just above the overlocking.) Thread the 3mm wide satin ribbon through the beading now.

Step 4

With the right sides of the coathanger fabric facing each other, pin around the raw edges. Mark the centre of the top of the coathanger with a pin. Leave a small opening here, $^1/_2$" (1cm) to push the hook of the coathanger through. Machine around the raw edge of the coathanger with $^3/_8$"(4mm) seam allowance. Do not machine along the lace edge. Make sure you go backwards and forwards with your sewing machine at the centre points so the stitching does not come undone when you poke the coathanger hook through. Turn the coathanger fabric to the right side through the open bottom section (the bottom section is where the lace is).

Slide the hook through the opening at the top of the coathanger and then slip it over the padded section of the coathanger. Pin together the back and front of the coathanger along the lace section. Hand sew the two bottom edges together under the lace. You have now completed your coathanger.

The Wedding Card

What a lovely way to complete this wedding set. This beautiful card will match the wedding cushion and the wedding coathanger. I am sure every bride would love to have this trio.

Requirements:

1 cardboard card with the heart shape already cut out for you
1 small piece of wadding
14" (35cm) of cream braid, (you might require more, depending on the size of your heart cutout)
1 gold plastic wedding ring
1 piece of cream satin 7" x 7" (18cm x 18cm). (I have allowed extra fabric so you can place the fabric in a small hoop)
1 piece of cream cotton voile 8" x 8" (20cm x 20cm)
A small amount of craft glue
Needles: Chenille No 18 & Crewel No 9
A small amount of small cream pearl beads.

Ribbons and Threads:

1 card of Bucilla silk ribbon 13mm wide No 1321 Ivory
1 card of Bucilla silk ribbon 4mm wide No 501 Off White
1 skein of Ecru DMC stranded thread.

Note:

All silk ribbon embroidery must be embroidered in a hoop. Use a Chenille No 18 needle for all the silk ribbon and a No 9 Crewel needle is for the fine embroidery, unless otherwise stated in your instructions. Only use 12″ (30cm) of ribbon, unless otherwise stated in your instructions. Please read your instructions very carefully.

Daisy and Buds

Step 1

Hand tack the cotton voile to the back of the satin fabric 1/2″ (1cm) in from the edge. It is a good idea to overlock or oversew the raw edges as the satin tends to fray.

Single Daisy

Step 2

Transfer your design as per Transferring Instructions. Only transfer a small section at any one time.

Step 3

Embroider the Carnations, Carnation leaves, Daisies, Daisy leaves and Daisy buds the same as the Wedding Cushion. The bow and ring are also the same as the Wedding Cushion.

Step 4

I did not embroider my initials on the card, instead I signed and dated the back of the card.

For Cushion and Coathanger

Heart Shape for Feather Stitch

How to Assemble the Wedding Card

Step 1

Glue the piece of wadding to the flat side of the card. This will give the embroidery a raised effect.

Step 2

Place the embroidered section over the opening on the wrong side of the card. You will have to trim some of the fabric away. Cut to size, making sure you leave some excess fabric. Glue the embroidered section to the inside of the card, Diagram 2. The embroidery will be facing the front of the card.

Step 3

When the embroidered section is dry, glue the embroidered front of the card to the back of the card (with the wadding on it). Hold firmly until the glue is dry. Clothes pegs make good clamps while the glue is drying.

Step 4

Glue the braid around the outline of the heart, on the right side of the card. The silk ribbon bow with the small gold ring on it will cover the join of the braid.

The Gold Pedestal
Vase of Flowers Cushion

This is a very different arrangement of flowers, but beautiful in its own special way. The colours are very different as well. Diamond flowers give a very special touch. The silk thread "fill in" flowers highlight the arrangement. I designed this variegated cream Kacoonda thread a few years ago with Kathy Bielney, because I love to work with tone on tone threads. The colour is known as No 4. This cushion is 11″ x 11″ (28cm x 28cm) without the frill.

Requirements:
1 piece of cream silk dupion 19$\frac{1}{2}$″ x 1yd 9″ (50cm x 115cm)
1 piece of cream cotton voile 13″ x 13″ (33cm x 33cm)
2 small diamantes
A small amount of cream small pearl beads
A small amount of Mill Hill frosted glass seed beads No 62024
1 gold pedestal
1 spring hoop 7″ (18cm) in diameter
Needles: Chenille No 18 & Crewel No 9 and 7
2yds 27″ (2.5 m) of cream cotton lace of your choice 1″ (2.5mm) wide. Note: this lace must have holes to thread the lace through

4yds 14″ (4 m) of 3mm wide double sided satin ribbon
1 cream 8″ (20cm) zip.

Ribbons and Threads:
1 card of Bucilla 7mm wide silk ribbon No 7101 Candlelight
1yd 4″ (1 m) of 4mm wide YLI silk ribbon No 179 Dark Grape
2 yds 8″ (2 m) of 4mm wide YLI silk ribbon No 178 Light Grape
1 hank of Kacoonda thick silk No 4 variegated Cream
Approximately a half a skein of the following DMC threads No 712 Cream, No 3041 Dark Grape, No 3042 Light Grape, No 523 Light Green, No 738 Light Fawn
A small amount of DMC No Art.273 Gold and Black Glitter.

Note:
   Make sure you embroider all silk ribbon in a hoop and use the Chenille No 18 needle for all silk ribbon, unless otherwise stated in your instructions. The No 9 Crewel is for the fine embroidery. Only use 12″ (30cm) of silk ribbon at any one time, unless more is stated in the instructions. Please read your instructions carefully.

Step 1

Hand tack the cotton voile to the back of the silk fabric $1/2''$ (1cm)in from the raw edge. It is a good idea to overlock or oversew the raw edges before you begin your embroidery.

Daisy and Buds

Step 2

Transfer your design as per Transferring Instructions. Only transfer a small section at a time.

Carnation

Step 3

Embroider the Carnations, using 7mm wide silk ribbon No 7101. Use one strand of No 712 for the Carnations. Please follow the separate instructions on how to embroider the Carnations. You will need 12″ (30cm) of silk ribbon per Carnation.

Step 4

Embroider the Carnation leaves, using two strands of stranded thread No 523. Each leaf is embroidered using two fly stitches on top of each other and one straight stitch in the centre of the last fly stitch.

Step 5

Embroider the loop stitch flowers. Each flower will use 12″ (30cm) of 4mm wide silk ribbon No 179. You must use the two needles at one time. The Chenille No

Loop Stitch Flower

18 needle is for the 4mm wide silk ribbon and the Crewel No 9 is for the catching down of each loop stitch petal. The No 9 Crewel needle will have one thread of No 3041 and this thread will be used to embroider one very small straight stitch in the centre of the silk ribbon petal (at the base of the petal) to prevent the loop pulling through.

Note: Always keep the needles on the top side of your embroidery because the ribbon and thread will become entangled in each other if the thread and ribbon are left on the underneath. Please check the separate instructions for the loop stitch flower. Hand sew the diamante in the centre of the loop stitch flower.

Ribbon Stitch Flowers

Step 6

Embroider the ribbon stitch flowers, using 4mm wide silk ribbon No 178. Embroider one small straight stitch in the centre of the ribbon stitch petal (at the base of the petal) with one thread of No 3042. Hand sew one glass seed bead in the centre of each flower using No 62024 seed beads.

Step 7

Embroider the cream silk thread Daisies, using Kacoonda thick silk No 4. Each Daisy has five even lazy daisy stitch petals. The Daisy buds are one lazy daisy stitch per bud using the same thread. Hand sew a small cream pearl bead in the centre of each Daisy. Embroider the Daisy leaves, using one strand of stranded thread No 523. Each leaf is one very small fly stitch. Embroider one fly stitch around

each bud and extend the holding stitch back to the Daisy to form the stem. Use the same thread as for the leaves.

Step 8

nots

Embroider the Rose buds, using two strands of stranded thread No 738. I use a No 9 Crewel needle for my bullion stitches, but if you would prefer another

Bullion Rose Buds

needle, the choice is yours. The buds are embroidered as follows. The centre bullion stitch of the bud has eleven twists. Embroider one bullion stitch either side of the centre bullion using nine twists. You might have to adjust your number of twists depending on your tension. My tension is quite tight. Embroider the greenery on the buds next. Bring the needle out just above the bud to the left of the centre bullion and slide the needle under the centre bullion but not through the fabric and take the needle into the fabric to the right of the centre bullion. Embroider one fly stitch around the bud, but do not extend the holding stitch. Embroider another fly stitch around the first fly stitch, this time extend the holding stitch back to the other flowers close by to form the stems. Each bud will be extended into a different flower, so please check your design sheet first. Some of the buds will have small lazy daisy leaves using one strand of stranded thread No 523. Extend the holding stitch on each leaf a little longer. Check your design for the leaf positions.

Step 9

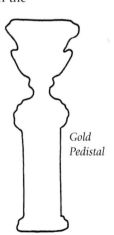

Lavender

Embroider the Lavender stems, using one strand of stranded thread No 523 and feather stitch. You must embroider the feather stitch from the outside in. Embroider the Lavender flowers next using two strands of stranded thread No 3042 and embroider a nine twist bullion stitch for each flower.

Step 10

Embroider the Forget-me-nots, using Kacoonda thick silk No 4. Each flower has four outside colonial knots embroidered very close together. Embroider the centre colonial knot using three strands of stranded thread No 738. Your Forget-me-nots might not be in exactly the same place as mine. Just fill in the spaces with Forget-me-nots.

Step 11

It is a good idea to initial and date your embroidery. Hand sew the pedestal in position now. Use DMC metallic thread No Art.273, as this thread is very similar in colour to the gold pedestal and the stitches will blend in with the pedestal. Catch one stitch either side of the top of the urn and then catch the two strands together with a loop along the top of the urn. This stitch will stop the thread falling off the end of the urn, otherwise there is nothing to hold the thread onto the urn. Embroider

Gold Pedistal

more straight stitches over the pedestal at the base of the urn, just below the first section of the pedestal and then at the bottom of the pedestal. You could glue the pedestal onto the fabric, but I do not like to use glue on a beautiful cushion like this.

STEP 12
Make your cushion up following the instructions from the Spray of Carnations Cushion. These two cushions are the same size. The frill on this cushion is different. The frill for this cushion has two lengths joined in a circle, but the frill is only 3.5″ x 1yd 9″ (9cm x 115cm). This frill is a single layer of fabric. Overlock both edges of the frill now. Machine the cotton lace onto the outside edge of the silk fabric. Now

follow the same instructions for the previous cushion. Once you have completed the machining on your cushion, you can thread the 3mm wide satin ribbon through the eyelets of the lace. Secure off the ends of the ribbon with a few overstitches. Cut three lengths of 3mm wide satin ribbon 19.5″ (50cm) long. Take all three pieces of ribbon and tie them together in a bow. Hand sew this bow at the join of the threaded ribbon. The bow will cover the join of the ribbon. Cut the bow's ribbon tails on the cross angle to finish off.

Illustration only

Pattern

Guide

**A Shoe Filled with Beautiful
Flowers Cushion**

Actual Size

The Australian Wildflower Framing

Enlarge by 33%

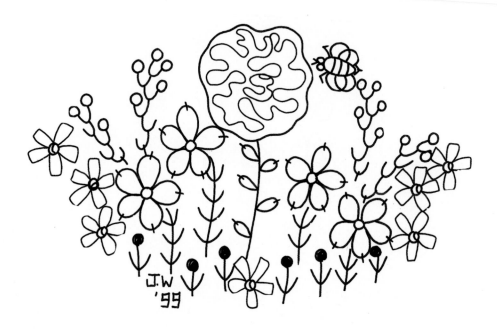

The Ruby Rose Pincushion

Actual Size

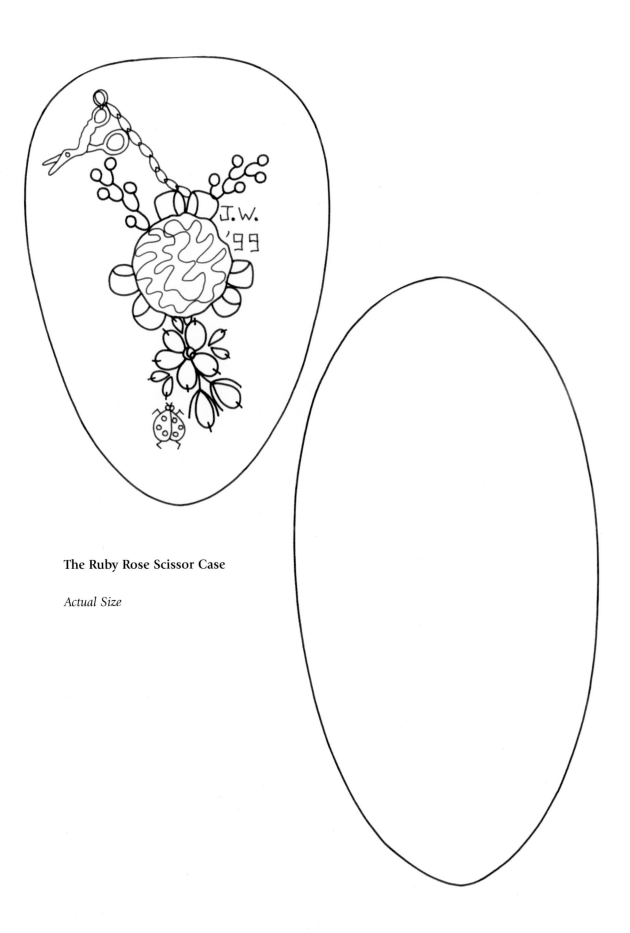

The Ruby Rose Scissor Case

Actual Size

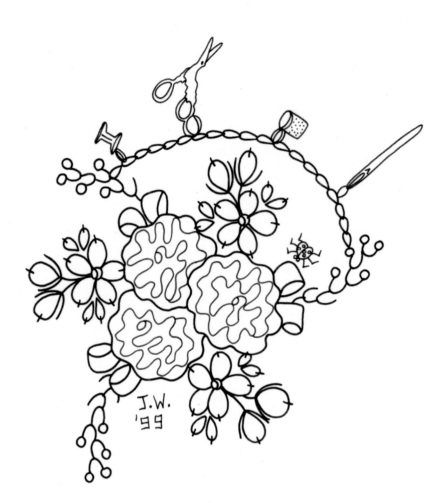

Pin Cushion

Actual Size

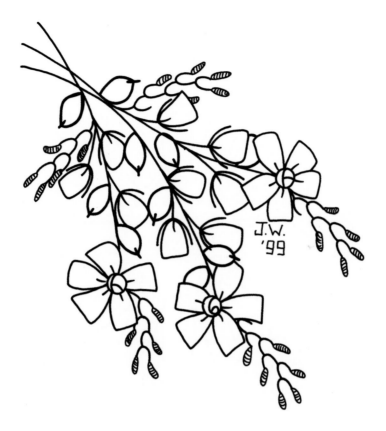

A Beautiful Lavender Bag

Actual Size

**A Pink Chrysanthemum
Lavender Bag**

Actual Size

**Large Framing with White
Daisies in a Cameo Vase**

Enlarge by 30%

The Elegance of the Cream Evening Bag

Actual Size

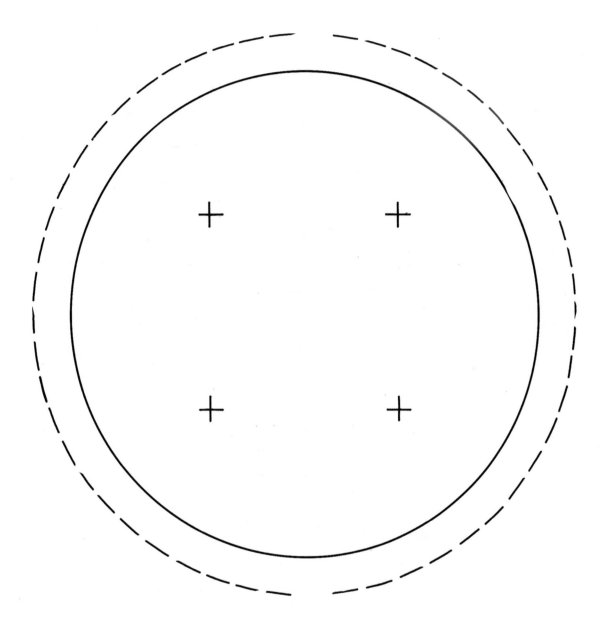

Evening Bag Base

Actual Size

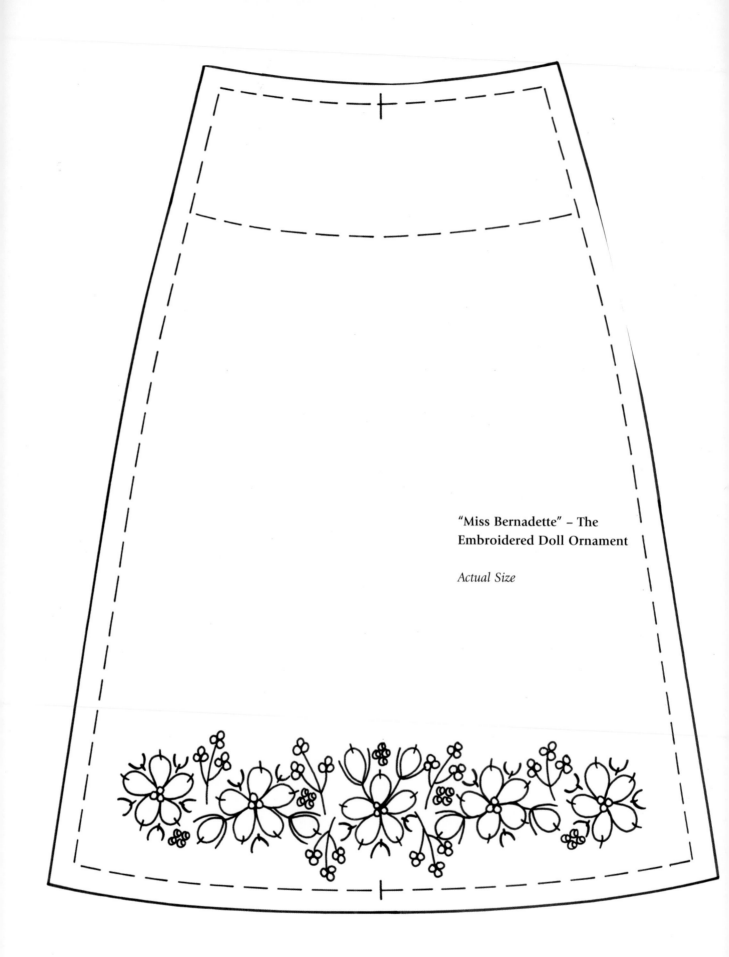

"Miss Bernadette" – The
Embroidered Doll Ornament

Actual Size

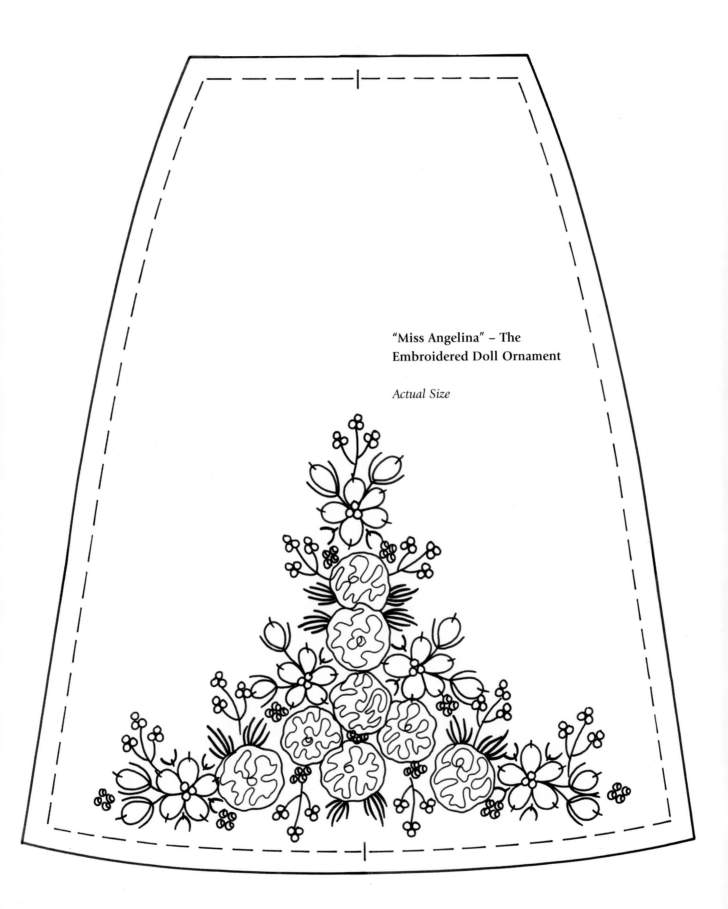

"Miss Angelina" – The
Embroidered Doll Ornament

Actual Size

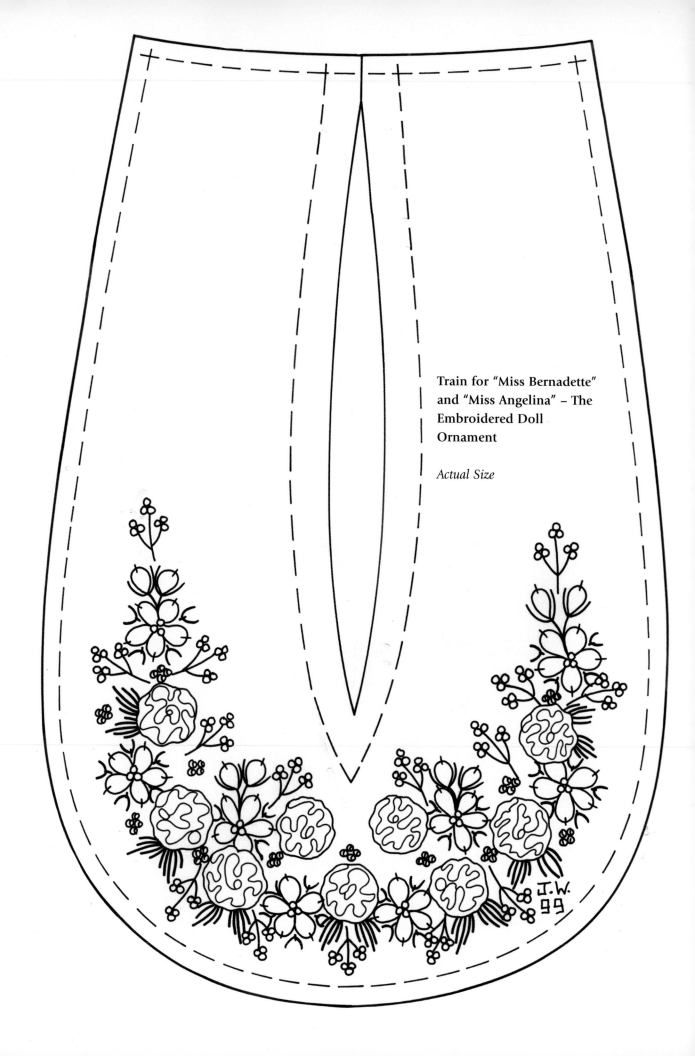

Train for "Miss Bernadette"
and "Miss Angelina" – The
Embroidered Doll
Ornament

Actual Size

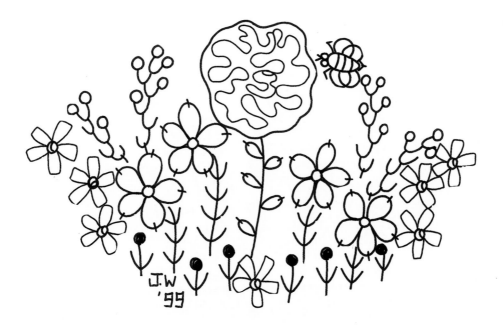

The Ruby Rose Garden Framing

Actual Size

The Hollyhock Garden
Framing

Actual Size

**The Sunflower and
Watering Can Cushion**

Enlarge by 30%

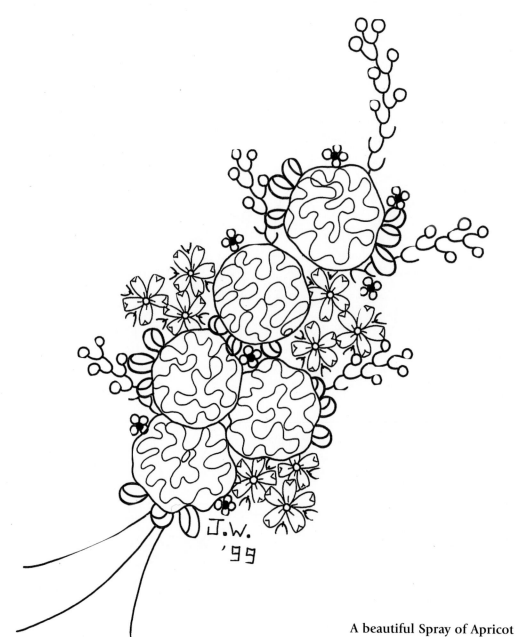

A beautiful Spray of Apricot
Carnations Cushion

Actual Size

The Wedding Card

Actual Size

The Wedding Cushion

Enlarge by 30%

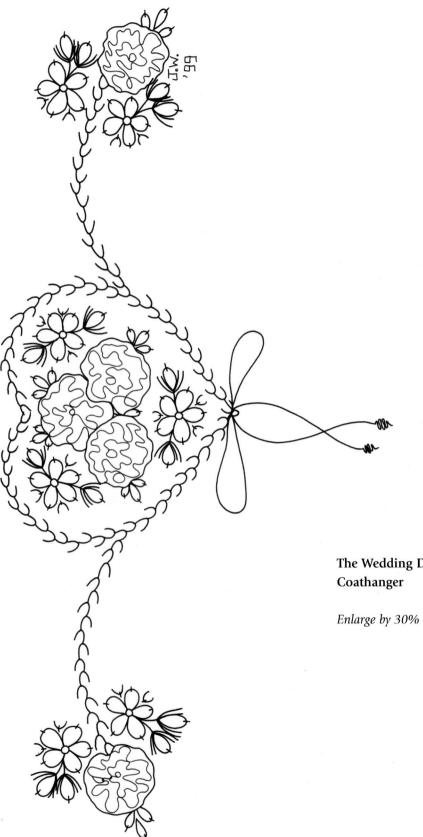

**The Wedding Dress
Coathanger**

Enlarge by 30%

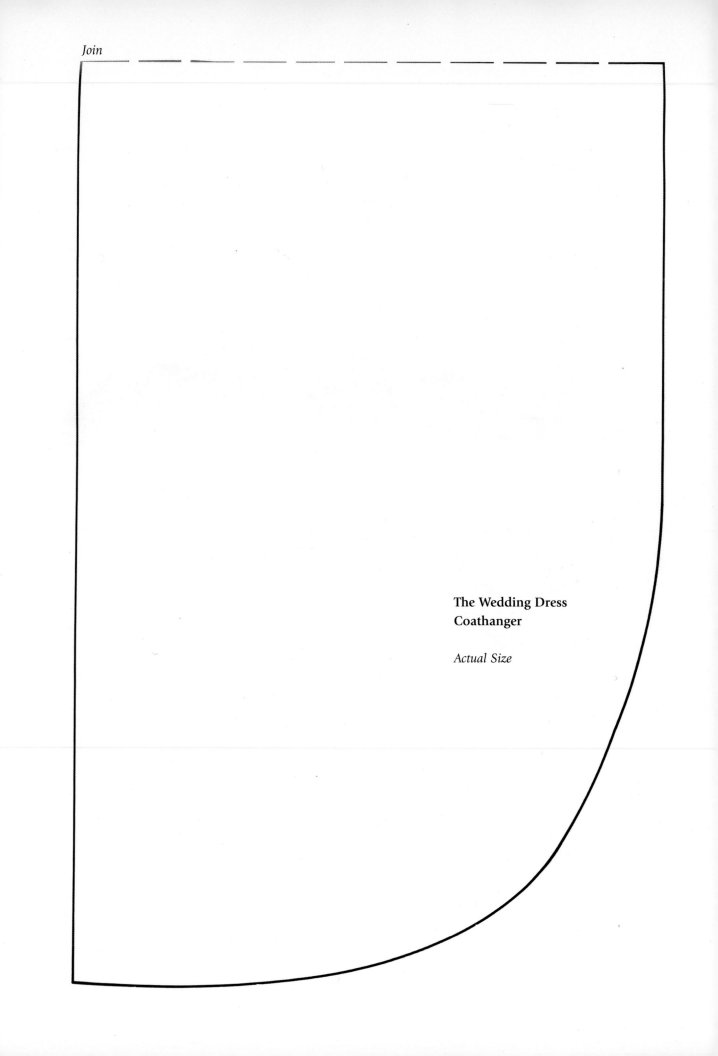

Join

**The Wedding Dress
Coathanger**

Actual Size

Join

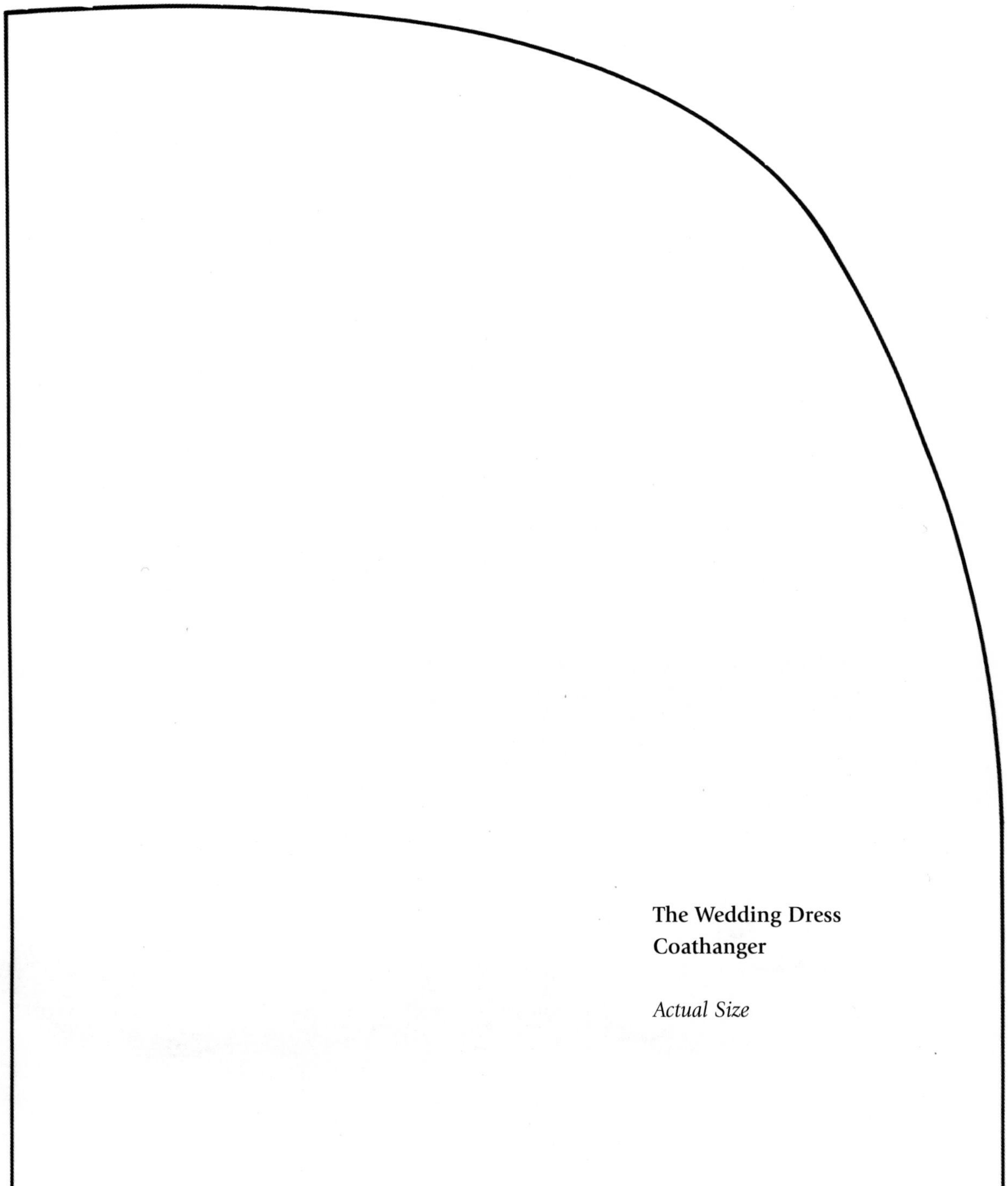

**The Wedding Dress
Coathanger**

Actual Size

Join

**The Gold Pedestal Vase
of Flowers Cushion**

Actual Size

J.W.
99